FOCUS
On Your
DREAM

How to Turn
Your Dreams
and Goals
Into *Reality*

Jeffrey D. Smith

Focus On Your Dream

Jeffrey D. Smith

Copyright©2002 by Jeff Smith

e-mail: stressfree@sprintmail.com

ISBN 0-938716-40-9

Published by

Possibility Press

e-mail: PossPress@aol.com

Cover Photo: Digital Imagery© copyright 2001 PhotoDisc, Inc.

Manufactured in the United States of America

DEDICATION

To My Mother, Alyce, I Love You!

ACKNOWLEDGEMENTS

I never could have written *Focus On Your Dream* without the help, inspiration, and guidance of my many teachers and mentors, as well as the love and support of my friends and family. I acknowledge those that made this book possible.

My mother, Alyce; father, David and his wife Dorothy; my brother, Tod, and his wife, Jeni; my grandparents, Catherine Rupp and Roy and Georgia Smith; Norma Butler; John Assaraf; the members of my Indianapolis Mastermind Group; Dr. Fred Grosse; Mike Fry; Shelley Stuteville; and the staff at Possibility Press.

Contents

Preface

"The only ones among you who will be really happy (and successful) are those who will have sought and found how to serve."
Albert Schweitzer

True meaning in life comes after you realize your own potential through personal growth and serving other people. Rushing after the "magic solutions" most people believe are "out there" is like running in quicksand. The more you struggle, the quicker you sink.

You were born with all the potential you need to accomplish your goals and live the life you want. What you need to do is *focus on your dream*, become aware of how to work with the talents you already have, and serve others to the best of your ability. Follow these three steps and you'll be on your way to realizing your dream...no matter how big it may be!

By the time you finish reading this book, you will have developed a refreshing new way of looking at the world and yourself.

- ♦ You will see more of the beauty of the world around you.
- ♦ You will enjoy the self-confidence that comes from knowing who you are and why you are here.
- ♦ You won't feel the need to continually compare yourself to other people.
- ♦ And, you will know how to turn your dream into reality, including the material wealth you may desire.

My hope is that this book will serve as a stepping stone to greater things in your life. That alone will have made my efforts here worthwhile.

If there is one thing I've learned over the years, it's that the fine line between those who win and those who don't is what they *focus on*. Winners *stay focused* on what they *want* and *continually take action* to move themselves closer to their dream. Everyone else doesn't.

Focus makes the difference between the World Champion and the also-ran. In this book, you'll learn how to develop the focus of a World Champion. Hopefully, it will inspire, motivate and most importantly, *activate* you into taking action—as you sharpen your focus on your dream. *So, let's get started...*

Introduction

Staying Focused On Success— The Basics

"The first law of success...is concentration: to blend all the energies to one point, and to go directly to that point, looking neither to the right nor the left."
William Matthews

Focus—*What Does It Really Mean?*

Undoubtedly you've heard the word "focus" time and time again. Yet, you may have never given it much thought or realized how essential this little five-letter word is to your success. Webster's New World Dictionary defines focus as, *"...to fix or settle on one thing; concentrate."*

Have you ever noticed that *you get what you focus on?* For example, when you drive your car to the grocery store, you need to steer it in the right direction, or you're just not going to get there, are you? Life's much the same. You're in the driver's seat of your life. You need to consistently focus your thinking and take action in a specific direction to make continuous progress toward your dream.

People who win in business or anything else, for that matter, focus and make things happen. They may look lucky, as if they just glided into a higher level of accomplishment without much effort. Instead though, they're usually like the serene-looking duck, smoothly crossing the lake.   Underwater, their little webbed feet are paddling consistently and vigorously toward their goal.   They're focused on reaching the shore so they can eat the bread you're tossing into the water!

What Questions Are You Asking Yourself?

In the process of staying *focused* and achieving your goals, the questions you ask yourself are at least as important, if not more so, than the answers you give!

You need to ask yourself powerful, focused questions to get the results you want. For example, *"What am I doing today to live my dream?"* Find the question that works the best for whatever you want to achieve, write it down, and put it up in several places where you'll see it every day. The quality of your life is affected by the questions you consistently ask yourself every day.

What Is Success?

Let's start our journey with a question: "What does success mean to you?"

If you're like most folks, that question may have challenged you. You may have pictured a beautiful new house, a shiny sportscar or luxury car, or being on a sun-drenched beach. You may have thought of your family, gathered around the dinner table smiling and laughing, enjoying each other's company and sharing a beautiful love that seems rare today.

You may even have pictured a large check coming to you in the mail on a regular basis—the kind of income that would give you the freedom you so desire.

All of those may be some of the *results* of your success, but they don't really define it. You need to have a clear definition of what success means to *you*. It's the only way for you to know what you're working toward and how to determine when you've achieved it. That makes sense, doesn't it?

Now, ask yourself the same question again: "What does success really mean to me?" Is your answer still the same? If not, what is it?

How Do Some Other Achievers Define Success?

Robert Louis Stevenson, author of *Treasure Island*, said... *"That man is a success who has lived well, laughed often and loved much; who has gained the respect of intelligent men and the love of children; who has filled his niche and accomplished his task; who leaves the world better than he found it, whether by an improved poppy, a perfect poem or a rescued soul; who never lacked appreciation of earth's beauty or failed to express it; who looked for the best in others and gave the best he had."*

Albert Einstein, one of the greatest scientists who ever lived said, *"A successful man is he who receives a great deal from his fellow man, usually incomparably more than corresponds to his service to them. The value of a man, however, should be seen in what he gives, and not in what he is able to receive."*

And, Earl Nightingale, author of *The Strangest Secret* and one of the most well-known motivational speakers of all-time, offered one of the most useful definitions of success: *"Success is the progressive realization of a worthy ideal."*

When you study each of those definitions, you'll begin to get a much clearer picture of what success really is. As you can see, none of these people defined success as lots of money or luxury cars or new homes. Those things are simply the *rewards* of success but, in and of themselves, they are not success.

Real Success Is Deeper

True success goes much deeper than material objects. As William H. Danforth said, *"Our most valuable possessions are those which can be shared without lessening; those which, when shared, multiply.   Our least valuable possessions are those which, when divided, are diminished."* Now that's certainly worth rereading. When you do, look for the powerful definition of the concept of success that's in it.

What Danforth means is that money and most of the things it buys are some of the *least* valuable possessions we have.   Ironically, most people spend the majority of their lives working for money at jobs they can't stand. Then they go into debt to buy material objects, which are actually some of the least valuable things in their lives. They seek instant gratification to ease the pain of working their jobs.

That doesn't make too much sense, yet almost everyone does it. Why? Many people simply believe they have to. Others may feel it's the right thing to do because "everyone else" is doing it. Still others do it because they think there is no other way.

Many people though, do it because they're trying to fill the gap they have between making a living and making a life. They are bored and unfulfilled—living in gray mediocrity. So they constantly seek "stuff," entertainment, and other things in an attempt to make up for what they're missing.

You don't have to be stuck in any of those traps. You can be different. You don't have to be average. It isn't the right thing to do just because everyone else is doing it. Fortunately, there is another way. That's what you'll learn in this book. You'll discover the path that allows you to achieve true success—*your success!*

You can drive your dream car, live in your dream home, and go on luxurious vacations. After all, you do need to be drawn by your dream to become successful. Things, in and of themselves however, aren't that important. *What's important is what you become along the way.* The wisdom, understanding and love for people you develop in order to achieve your dream is really what it's all about.

When you help enough people succeed, you'll be wealthy in many ways—not just money-wise. The wisdom, understanding, and love are the possessions that *"when shared, multiply."* They are the essence of true success and fulfillment.

The question you probably have now is, "Okay, Jeff, I've got a pretty good understanding of what success really means to me. But doesn't it take tons of hard work, blood, sweat, and tears to ever achieve the level of success where I can make all my dreams come true? How can I ever do it with all that's going on in my life?

That's where *focus* comes in—and that's what we'll focus on in the rest of this book. *Now let's start sharpening our focus.*

Chapter 1

What's Your Starting Point?

"Do what you can, with what you have, where you are."
Teddy Roosevelt

Where Are You Now?

The first thing you need to know before you focus on your dream is where you're starting from. Fill in the list below to help you determine that.

Give yourself a score of 1 to 10 in the following areas: your health, family life, relationships, spirituality, social life, business, personal development, education, income, and financial situation (assets, liabilities, retirement plan, and such.) Thinking about each of these areas of your life will give you a basic starting point for our next discussion.

Key Life Areas	Where Am I?	Where Would I Like To Be?
Health		
Family Life		
Relationships		
Spirituality		
Social Life		

Key Life Areas	Where Am I?	Where Would I Like To Be?
Career		
Business		
Personal Development		
Education		
Income		
Financial Situation		

Imagine yourself waking up one morning in an unfamiliar place and saying, "I'd like to get out of here." The problem is, without knowing where you are starting from and what your destination is, you obviously would have no clue which direction to go. Even if you are totally determined to get somewhere, you'll spend the rest of your life just wandering around going nowhere!

Most people lead their lives out of focus. They wander around, trying to get somewhere, without really knowing where they're starting from, where they want to go, or how to get there.

Starting now, promise yourself you won't be part of the "that's how most of us do it" *wandering* majority. You'll be different. You'll know where you're coming from and where you're going to. You'll be *focused.* Affirm to yourself, *"I am focused."*

Focus alone will make your journey more exciting and fun than anything you've ever experienced. There's exhilaration in focusing, pursuing and achieving your dream.

Now, let's begin by finding out exactly where you are today. Let's do a quick assessment of your situation.

Set up a worksheet like those on the previous two pages to help you think through this. Look back at what you've just written and ask yourself these questions:

- ♦ What areas of my life do I feel the most successful in?
- ♦ What areas do I feel need the most work?
- ♦ What areas are the furthest from where I'd like to be a year from today?
- ♦ What areas are the furthest from where I'd like to be 10 years from today?

Your answers to these questions are your starting points for becoming truly focused and successful in your life.

You now know, in general terms, where you're starting from. Your next steps are to decide where you want to go, determine how to get there, and to stay focused while you're doing whatever it takes.

Chapter 2

The *"You"* Factor

"Dream lofty dreams, and as you dream, so shall you become. Your vision is the promise of what you shall at last unveil."
John Ruskin

What Is the *"You"* Factor?
The next step in getting focused is to understand the *"You"* Factor, one of the most important aspects of this book. The *"You"* Factor has three main parts:

- ♦ How you basically function.
- ♦ Why you are where you are.
- ♦ How you can achieve different results in your life.

The *"You"* Factor, Part I—*How Do You Basically Function?*
Before you can determine why you are where you are and how to get somewhere else, it first helps to have a basic understanding of what you have to work with. You are primarily made up of three components:

- ♦ Your physical body.
- ♦ Your mind—both conscious and sub-conscious.
- ♦ Your spiritual nature.

Your Physical Body

This is the most obvious part of your nature. To draw an analogy, imagine you are a computer with all its hardware and accessories. You need to take care of your body's health or it will be harder for you to do whatever it takes to make your dreams come true. And without good health, not much else will matter to you.

Your Mind—*Conscious and Subconscious*

Your conscious mind is your intellect, which is where you think and make decisions. In our analogy, this is where you decide to either load in new software or leave things as they are.

Your subconscious mind does not think. It takes and follows orders given to it by your conscious mind. It doesn't make judgments, it only takes what it is given, positive or negative. It's like the hard drive in your computer where all the memory is held. It takes all the "programming"—images and beliefs—of your life, that result in your habits and actions.

The great thing is, it can be "reprogrammed" to move you in the direction of your dream, depending on what "software" you install. In your conscious mind you decide what to do. You either load a new program to get new results, or let the old program in so you can keep getting the same old results.

Focusing on your dream and taking action is like loading "dream software" into your computer and putting it to use. This is basically how you can break out of any "ruts" you may be in and create major changes in your life.

Your Spiritual Nature

This is the third part of your nature. You were created for a purpose, just like your computer was designed in a specific way to perform certain tasks. And even though you can't see your spiritual nature, it is the source of your dream.

Faith, which is belief in things unseen, inspires you to have a dream. It gives you a vision, which leads to a greater understanding of why you were put here on this earth. It is essential for true happiness and success, which are the results of fulfilling your purpose.

Life is really about serving others. And when you help enough other people—in line with your purpose—success, happiness, and fulfillment will follow.

The *"You"* Factor, Part II—*Why Are You Where You Are?*

The second part of the *"You"* Factor is understanding how the body, mind and spiritual components of your nature work together to determine the results you get in your life. Here's how:

♦ You are guided and inspired by your spiritual nature.

♦ You consciously have thoughts or unconsciously allow thoughts to enter your mind.

♦ These thoughts create an image which enters your subconscious mind.

♦ Your subconscious mind cannot reason or change the image or idea it receives, so it accepts exactly what is given to it. If enough similar images are placed into the subconscious, you will develop a belief or habit based on them. This is called *conditioning*. It is a major factor in determining how you look at yourself and the world around you, as well as how focused you are.

♦ You then begin to experience feelings based on the images that have been given to your subconscious mind. The strongest images and ideas—your strongest conditioning—will create the strongest feelings.

♦ Next, you take action based on the feelings you are having.

♦ Finally, the actions you take determine the results you get.

You can remember how this process works by thinking *ITIFAR*. You are *Inspired* to create *Thoughts* which form *Images* which lead to *Feelings* that determine your *Actions* which give you your *Results*. Work backwards through this process and you'll be able to understand why you are where you are today as follows:

- ◆ You have a certain set of present results.
- ◆ These results are directly attributable to the actions you have taken.
- ◆ These actions have depended on the feelings you were experiencing.
- ◆ These feelings were caused by the images accepted by your subconscious mind.
- ◆ The images in your subconscious mind were formed by thoughts, which you either consciously chose or unconsciously allowed to enter your conscious intellectual mind.
- ◆ You were guided and inspired by your spiritual nature.

If the results you presently have in your life aren't exactly what you'd like them to be, you now have a better idea of how that happened. At the beginning of this cycle, you either chose negative thoughts or somehow allowed them to enter your mind.

These thoughts then put images into your subconscious which, over time, took root and grew into your beliefs and habits. (This would be your conditioning or "programming.") These negative habits and beliefs created negative emotions, which led you to take the actions that created the results you do not want anymore.

Keep in mind that when I say negative thoughts or habits, I mean negative only in the sense that they are not leading to the new results you would like to have in your life.

The *"You"* Factor, Part III—*How Can You Achieve Different Results in Your Life?*

The most exciting thing you now understand is how to *change* the results you are presently getting in your life to any *different* results you would like to get. Here's how:

♦ Get inspired through your spiritual nature.

♦ Consciously choose a different, more effective, set of thoughts. *Focus* on thoughts of what you want, not on what you don't want.

♦ These thoughts will create a new set of images in your subconscious mind. As they are strengthened, your subconscious will go to work to help you turn those new images into physical reality.

♦ You'll experience a different set of feelings.

♦ Your new feelings will lead you to a different set of actions that are in line with the new images you have put into your subconscious mind.

♦ And, of course, these new actions will lead you to a new, more desirable set of results in your life—your dream.

Before we move on, here's one final reminder about expecting instant results. Don't! If you were having a new house built, you wouldn't expect it to be done the day after you handed the blueprints to your builder, would you? If you started on an exercise program, you wouldn't expect to be in tip-top shape in two days now, would you?

The same holds true for creating new and different results in your life. It's impossible to know how strong your negative conditioning, which is in your subconscious, has been over the years. You have no idea how many thoughts and experiences contributed to strengthening it. Therefore, you don't know how much time or effort it will take to change it! What you do know, however, is that when you *focus on your dream* and keep taking action, you will eventually achieve it.

Chapter 3

Decide And Focus On Where You Want To Be

"Obstacles are those frightful things you see when you take your eyes off your goal."
Henry Ford

Are You Dreamin' in Color But Livin' in Black and White?

Now you're ready to move on and start making the adjustments necessary to live your dream. The first step is for you to decide exactly what your dream is.

As the ever-inspiring baseball "philosopher" Yogi Berra once said, *"You've got to be very careful if you don't know where you're going because you might not get there."*

Knowing exactly where *you* want to go is essential to your success. Most people spend their entire lives pursuing someone else's dreams. They go to their graves "with their music still in them, their song unsung," because they never went for their own goals and dreams.

Make a promise to yourself that "From this moment on, I joyfully choose *my own* dream, pursue *my own* goals, and fulfill *my own* potential." Now, if you have a job, which you probably do, you still need to support your boss's goals, or you're likely to be out of that job. Yet, you can still pursue your dream outside of your job. Eventually you can move on from your job, if you choose to. Everyone has different talents and interests—different dreams. And if you have a family, you will be considering their needs and wants, too.

As you start the exciting process of *focusing*, keep in mind the "Principle of the Blank Page." From this moment forward, your life is like a blank page. *Nothing* that has happened to you in the past has to affect you today, unless you choose to let it! You are the writer of your own life script. You can create any kind of plot for your present and future that you choose. It's totally up to you. Best of all, you don't have to worry about a producer or anyone else editing your script. Whatever script you write is guaranteed to come true, provided you act it out *exactly* as you write it.

Focus on What You Want—*Not What You Already Have*

First you need to decide what your dream is. And, don't fall into the common trap of basing your expectations on what you already have. You need to be thankful for what you've already become and have accomplished, but don't rest on your laurels. If you focus on the present, you'll just get more of the same. Remember—*you get what you focus on.*

How much time do you spend focusing on what you don't want or don't like? Do you ever think about the negative parts of your job or your boss, challenges with the kids or your spouse, or the aches and pains you have? Every time you think about them you're simply reinforcing their images in your subconscious. This solidifies the beliefs, habits and conditioning that led to your present results.

If you are having the same feelings you've always had, you'll continue doing the same things you've always done. Consequently, you keep getting the same results. Remember, the subconscious accepts whatever you consistently dwell on and it keeps or makes it a reality. Constantly thinking about what you don't want would be creating a vicious circle. You'd be virtually guaranteeing yourself the same old results you'd like to change! The only way out of this mess is to— *focus on your dream.*

From Reactive to Creative

In effect, by focusing on your present results and letting them dominate your thinking, you have almost guaranteed the only thing you will get is more of the same. Focusing on what you *want*, instead of on what you already have, breaks this loop. You then shift from being reactive to being creative. Remember this definition of *insanity*— "continuing to do the same things while expecting *different* results!"

You need to consciously choose different input for your subconscious at the top of this whole cycle. When your mind is focused on your dream, images of it are going into your mind. This creates a reservoir of new mental pictures in your subconscious. It will then go to work to do the only thing it can—drive you to turn those images into reality.

Over time, as you solidify the new images in your subconscious and break down the old ones, you'll begin experiencing new feelings. This will lead you to take new actions which will bring you the new results you're looking for. You are then creating the life you want, rather than re-playing the same old scenes over and over again.

This is why goal setting and visualizing are so important and why virtually every single winner in life engages in them on a daily basis. As Albert Einstein once said, *"Imagination is more important than knowledge."*

Every time you set a goal or visualize your dream, you are consciously choosing to focus on a positive thought. You can then take the next step and deposit this into your subconscious so that you are developing new images that lead to new beliefs and habits (conditioning). They *naturally* cause you to feel a new set of emotions and take a different set of actions which lead to a new, more desirable set of results.

Take the Lid Off and Dream!

Now it's time to get crystal clear about your *dream* and the kind of life you *really* want to live. When you do, you can start turning that dream into reality. Get out a sheet of paper and invest 15 minutes answering these questions. Assume you're describing your *dream*. Don't let the present results in your life have anything to do with this. Let yourself go and have some fun!

- If time and money were no object, what would you do more of? Less of?
- If you could be the best in the world at any one thing, what would it be? *Why?*
- If you received $10,000,000 right now, what three things would you do with it and how much would those things cost?
- What is your perfect vacation? How long? With whom? To where? What would you do there?
- If you're single and want to be married, what would your ideal spouse be like? Would you have children? How many?
- Would you like to spend more time with your family? What would you most enjoy doing together? How would these relationships ideally be?
- If you could live anywhere in the world and bring your friends and family with you, where would it be?
- If you could learn one new skill and knew you would become an expert at it, what would it be?
- If you could change one thing about your life, what would it be?
- If you could change one thing about yourself, what would it be?

- If you knew you could not fail, what would you be doing each day? What hobbies or sports would you pursue? In what way would that affect how you build your dream? What kind of relationships would you build?
- If you could have any car ever built, what make and model would you drive?
- How much do you *really want* to earn each year? How many hours would you invest to create that income? What could you do, if anything, that you're not doing now to make it happen?
- *Exactly* what would you spend this money on? What would your house look like? How many rooms? How would it be decorated? What other things would you buy? Would you contribute to causes that are important to you? If so, which ones?

Make Your Dream Wants List

Now that you've started thinking in terms of what you *want,* instead of what you have or think you can get, make a master list of *all the wants* in your dream.

Have some fun with this. Get out your pen right now and invest 15 minutes brainstorming all the things *you* would like to experience in your dream. Aim to have at least 50 things on your list at the end of the 15 minutes. This is not the time for censoring yourself. *Whatever* pops into your mind, write it down, no matter how crazy or unlikely you think it is to happen.

Here are a few examples from my list that may help you get started:

- Wake up to the crisp mountain air coming in the windows of my Tahoe retreat.
- Invite my friends over to my own private island.
- Build my dream home and office complex on a lake overlooking the mountains.
- Build my own *"Field of Dreams"* baseball stadium in my backyard.

- Bench press 400 pounds.
- Have my own art exhibit at an art gallery.
- Help a homeless person start their own business and buy a house.
- Shoot hoops with world-famous basketball player, now retired, Michael Jordan.
- Write a *New York Times* #1 bestseller.
- Ride a gondola through Venice.
- Study with the world's top martial arts masters.
- Successfully build a foundation to teach the principles in this book to students, the homeless, the uneducated, single moms, and other groups who could really benefit from them.

The Next Two Components of Your Dream

If you've answered those questions faithfully, you now have a pretty good picture of what your physical world will be like in your dream.

Now you need to consider what kind of person you wish to become along the way to achieving it, by answering these four questions:

- What kind of person will you have become in your dream?
- How will people describe you?
- Imagine your local newspaper is writing a story about you. What would you like it to say about the kind of person you are and the things you have accomplished?
- If you could have one wish and you knew it would come true, what would it be? (You may not wish for more wishes!)

If you're having trouble deciding on your answers, close your eyes for a minute and imagine yourself at a large convention center. You are walking across stage to the thunderous standing ovation of the entire audience. People are beating on chairs, chanting, and clapping loudly to show their support and appreciation for what you've done. What wish comes to mind?

Did you just go to one of the top achievement levels in your field of endeavor? Did you end world hunger? Contribute a large sum to your favorite charity? Start a foundation to teach kids how to read? Raise the happiest, most loving family in the world? Lead your church successfully into new growth? Or inspire and motivate thousands at a seminar with the story of how you overcame your obstacles and made your dreams come true?

Your answer to this question will tell you a lot about what direction you should be going in your life. Think about what percentage of your life *today* is taken up with activities that directly contribute to accomplishing what you went across stage for. If my guess is right, it's probably very small.

For example, say your dream is to get out of debt and become financially free so you have the time and money to achieve other big dreams. How serious are you? Are you now investing the time and energy necessary to make it happen?

Don't criticize yourself, though. Remember the "Principle of the Blank Page"—from this moment forward, your life is a blank page and you can do anything with it you want. You can now begin doing whatever it takes, step by step. Eventually, you'll be recognized for your achievements as you progressively realize your dream. Remember—*you get what you focus on, and what you consistently take action on to achieve.*

If you've never gone through an exercise like this, you may have found it tough to answer some of these questions. That is quite common, so don't be concerned about it. You may have been receiving messages like: you can't have this or you can't do that, for most of your life! They have become firmly entrenched in your subconscious, and it will take some effort to overcome them. However, don't get discouraged. Stick with this because it is vitally important to your success. After all, this is *your* life that you're designing and what could be more important than that?

Remember *ITIFAR*? You are *Inspired* to have *Thoughts* that affect the *Images* in your subconscious, which affect your *Feelings* that lead to your *Actions*, that give you your *Results*. Investing some time in exercises like these is breaking up the old *Images* that are not leading to the new *Feelings*, *Actions* and *Results* that you want.

By picturing exactly what your dream is, you are consciously choosing positive Thoughts. You can then use them to create positive Images that will lead to positive Feelings and Actions, and finally to the positive Results you dream of. As Lewis Timberlake says in his book *Born to Win*, "An imagined experience is vividly recorded on the subconscious forever."

Build Your Own *Dreambuilding Book*

Once you have your lists of what your dream is, you need a place to keep them. You'll want to refer to them regularly and begin building the images in your mind that will lead to their realization. This is a part of dreambuilding—*focusing on your dream.*

One very effective way of doing this is to create a *Dreambuilding Book.* I have done this for years and it's been a lot of fun, as well as a wonderful tool to guide me down the road to my dream. A *Dreambuilding Book* is a book you create about everything you want in your life.

I simply started with a three-ring binder and a box of clear, plastic pages. Take photos of things you like or have someone else take a picture of you beside it or in it—like you in your dream car. Whenever I see pictures of the things I want in my life, I cut them out and put them in the plastic pages of my *Dreambuilding Book.*

I include pictures of places to visit, the new house I would build, artwork I like, people I would meet, causes I would contribute time or money to, books to read, and other things I would like to experience. Here is one possible "Table of Contents" for your own *Dreambuilding Book*.

- ◆ Places I will travel.
- ◆ Things I will experience.
- ◆ People I will meet.
- ◆ Things I will own (house, cars, boats, planes, clothes, and the like).
- ◆ Goals I will accomplish.
- ◆ My dream day, week, month, and year.
- ◆ My dream mental, emotional, spiritual, and physical state.
- ◆ What I will contribute to the world.
- ◆ What causes I will help and how I will help them.
- ◆ A list of books to read and knowledge I will acquire.
- ◆ My Dream.
- ◆ My Life's Mission or Focus Statement.
- ◆ What I will become.

Remember, this is *your Dreambuilding Book* of *your* dream. It needs to contain those pictures and statements that are meaningful to *you*. If you enjoy traveling, include places to travel in your book. If your church is one of the major focuses in your life, create an entire section related to it.

The bottom line is, customize your *Dreambuilding Book* so *you* get excited and emotionally involved with it every time you open it. That's the key to making *your* book an effective part of your plan for creating your dream.

Chapter 4

Develop A Solid Foundation For Achieving Your Goals

"If one advances confidently in the direction of his dreams, and endeavors to live the life which he has imagined, he will meet with a success unexpected in common hours."
Henry David Thoreau

Your Life's Focus

By now, it's likely you have a pretty good idea of what your dream will look like. It's time to determine what broad direction you want your life to move in. What kind of person do you need to become in order to live the dream? One good way to do this is to write your life's "Focus Statement," also called your statement of purpose, or mission statement.

You've probably heard all kinds of "talk" about mission statements and their importance. But if you're like most people, you really don't have a good idea about what a focus or mission statement is. You may not even realize why you need a mission statement, or how to develop one.

Why You Need a Life's *Focus Statement*

Your focus statement is your guide to help you stay on track so you can fulfill your potential and live your dream.

It's a simple benchmark you can use every day as you decide what actions to take to stay in line with your primary focus. It also serves as the "yardstick" you need to measure yourself with. You can then adjust and, if you've gone off course, get back on the path toward living your dream.

Having a clearly defined mission simplifies your decision making process. It serves as a guiding principle that helps you choose among alternative courses of action.

For example, part of my mission statement is "to be an example of maximum personal excellence." At times, I just feel like saying "the heck with it" and curling up on the couch for a nice afternoon nap. When I'm in this mood, I just ask myself this key question, "Would a person with the mission of becoming 'an example of maximum personal excellence' fritter the afternoon away on the couch? Or would they push themselves a little bit and finish their activities for the day?" Obviously, they would finish their tasks, so that's exactly what I do. The funny thing is, when I view my decisions in this way, it seems perfectly natural to finish my daily task list instead of taking a nap. Completing them is an action in harmony with my focus and mission. Taking a nap is not!

What Activities Contribute to Your Focus?

Focus or mission statements can also help you decide what to pursue and what to give up. For example, the second part of my mission is to "create opportunities for others to enjoy maximum personal excellence, growth, success, happiness, fulfillment, and understanding." Obviously, there are many ways to accomplish this.

I used to own a successful marketing consulting business. I realized, though, that some of my activities in that business did not lead to effective fulfillment of my mission. Yes, through doing those things I did help others build their businesses. Indirectly, they were "creating opportunities for others to enjoy growth, happiness, and fulfillment." But, on the other hand, I believed there was another way that would allow me to fulfill my mission even better.

My commitment to my mission made it easier for me to give up most of my marketing clients. I wasn't concerned about the temporary dip in my personal income or the emotions I would experience by shifting my career focus. By investing more of my time and resources in writing and speaking, I would be fulfilling my mission more effectively.

When I made this decision, I found that a lot of energy was released that had been bottled up inside me. I had been doing things solely because I was naturally good at them and they made money. Instead, I could have been doing things that contributed more to living my values and my mission. And, in the long run, I'd make more money anyway.

What about destiny? At this point, many people ask me, "You're sitting there telling me I have all this control over most everything in my life but sometimes I have trouble believing it. Sometimes it seems as if things just happen—as if there is some kind of pre-destiny that is determining what goes on in my life independently of my thoughts or decisions. Is there such a thing as destiny and how does it affect what I accomplish?" That's a very good question. The answer is, your destiny is up to *you!*

Imagine you are a painter ready to create a mural titled, *The Dream Fulfilled.* You sit in front of your canvas and get all your paints arranged. You have some great ideas and you're excited about getting started. You look up at the canvas and your mouth drops. You forgot you had casually put a series of broad brush strokes across it a few days earlier. You know there isn't a single other blank canvas that large in the entire city, and you're fired up to get moving on *The Dream Fulfilled.* You now have a decision to make.

You can choose to accept the broad brush strokes that are already there and work them into your painting. You'd then be creating a complete work of art from the few broad strokes you had to start with. Or, you can say, "Yuck, I've changed my mind. Those colors and patterns are ugly and I don't like them." In that case, you would paint over them and completely change the picture. It's your painting and your decision. You could decide to work with the broad strokes that are already there or paint over them and create an entirely new picture from scratch.

That's the role destiny plays. What we sometimes call destiny can be thought of as a broad brush stroke. It may say that you have a tendency to be better at athletics, you have a natural gift for speaking, or you have a brilliant mind for numbers. Those are the broad brush strokes. It's up to you whether you incorporate them into your *The Dream Fulfilled* or leave them out and use a whole new approach.

You make the decision about whether or how to use your broad brush strokes. Just because you can outrun everyone you know, doesn't mean you have to become an Olympic sprinter. You are perfectly free to invest your time into getting out of debt, building wealth, and advancing in your business or profession in any direction you choose.

Focus Vs. Mission

There's a special reason why I called this section your Life's Focus or mission statement.

Many people think of a mission statement as a permanent thing they must rigidly follow forever. Often, it's easier to think in terms of your Life's Focus. You choose what you would like to focus your life on today, based on your current level of awareness. If you later reach a point where you become aware of a new direction, you are free to change your Life's Focus to reflect your new awareness.

The process you're going through, as you read this book, will help you make that decision. Just stay relaxed and your decision will make itself clear to you.

And, remember, you are the one doing the painting. Your *The Dream Fulfilled* is your creation. There is no right or wrong way to paint your masterpiece. If you don't like part of it, just go back and paint over it.

How Can You Create Your Life's *Focus Statement?*

Start with answering this one simple question: *"What am I willing to dedicate my life to?"*

Think about that for a moment. What are you really willing to dedicate your life to? Helping to spread free enterprise? Eliminating world hunger? Finding a cure for cancer? Making others laugh and smile? Helping people achieve financial independence? Getting out of debt and providing the lifestyle your family deserves?

I recently read a story about Mother Teresa, a woman who did a tremendous amount of charitable work in her lifetime. The reporter had asked her why she did what she did. She said simply that her mission was to help others die more peacefully. And that's what she focused her entire life on. Her focus helped her to be quite successful and fulfilled, while making a real difference in the world.

Now get a sheet of paper and begin sketching ideas for your life's mission. Don't expect to hit on your "dream" Life's Focus immediately. Just jot down ideas and play with them until you have something that feels right to *you*. It took me almost two years of working with my focus statement before I had it phrased exactly the way I wanted it!

Here's how to create your own *Focus Statement:*

♦ Answer the question, "What am I willing to dedicate my life to?"

- ◆ Imagine yourself in a large convention hall. You're going across stage. What have you done to cause the crowd to cheer so loudly?
- ◆ Remember answering the question earlier about what one wish you would choose if you could have any wish you wanted? What did your answer tell you about what you feel is really important? What kind of Life's Focus statement might support this feeling? How can you achieve this focus?

Take ten minutes and brainstorm answers to these three questions. When you're done, it's likely you'll have a good sense of at least the general area for your mission or life's purpose. To help you with phrasing your mission and focus in a way that is meaningful to you, here are some starters:

- ◆ My mission is to teach others to _____ .
- ◆ My mission is to learn and to grow _____ .
- ◆ The focus of my life is to provide_____ for _____ .
- ◆ The focus of my life is to make a difference by _____ .

When you have a focus statement that feels right to you, write it several times on several clean sheets of paper. Put one on your desktop, your refrigerator, your bathroom mirror, or some other place where you'll see it regularly. Take the last copy and add it to your *Dreambuilding Book.*

Review your focus or mission statement at least once a day until it is ingrained in your mind. Keep revising it until it's worded the way you want it. Make a commitment to *focus* on living your mission daily.

When you are making decisions, ask yourself, "What would a person with my mission and focus do in this situation?" Then do it, joyously, and without hesitating, because you know it is the right decision for *you.*

The next few steps may make you feel a bit uncomfortable at first...doing some of the things you need to do to fulfill your mission. But soon you'll look forward to breaking out of your comfort zone daily. Here's something to inspire you:

Breaking Out Of Your Comfort Zone

"I used to have a comfort zone where I knew I couldn't fail.
The same four walls and busywork
were really more like jail.
I longed so much to do the things I'd never done before,
But I stayed inside my comfort zone and
paced the same old floor.

I said it didn't matter that I wasn't doing much.
I said I didn't care for things like diamonds, cars and such,
I claimed to be so busy with the things inside the zone,
But deep inside I kept longing for some victory of my own.

I couldn't let my life go by just watching others win!
I held my breath and stepped outside
to let the change begin.

I took a step and with new strength I'd never felt before,
I kissed my comfort zone goodbye and
closed and locked the door.

If you are in a comfort zone afraid to venture out,
Remember that all winners at one time were filled with
similar doubt. A step or two and words of praise can
make your dreams come true. Greet your future with a smile —
success is there for you."
Author Unknown

Chapter 5

Focus On Beliefs That Will Help You Win

"Things do not change, we change."
Henry David Thoreau

Develop Success-Inducing Beliefs

When you get inspired and keep putting success-inducing thoughts into your mind, they will produce success-inducing images. They lead to the emotions and actions necessary to achieve your goals and dreams.

Instead of "garbage in/garbage out," you'll have "Thoughts of a winner in/actions of a winner out." Of course, *that winner is you!* The way to make this process easy and natural is to adopt guiding beliefs that are productive and empowering, instead of destructive and limiting.

Incorporating Empowering Beliefs into Your Life

We all hold slightly different beliefs based on our culture, our conditioning, and other influences in our lives. Think for a minute about what beliefs you have in these areas:

- Spiritual or religious.
- Personal business and relationships, including family.
- Money and finances.
- Career, including your business.
- Health and exercise.

Get out a piece of paper and jot down what you believe in each of these areas. Be honest with yourself. Your beliefs are a primary component of your actions, which create the results in your life.

Therefore, *you can easily tell what your beliefs are by looking at the results you are getting.*

Invest a few minutes thinking about this. It will help you understand yourself better. Think about the beliefs you already have, which created the results in your life, which may or may not be serving you. You may believe something, but often times another, more comfortable belief you hold overrides and negates it.

For example, even if you are overweight, you still may not believe that eating low-fat foods is important. Or even though you might believe a low-fat diet is healthy, you may have a stronger belief that you deserve to indulge in high-fat snacks every day.

Here are the four keys to help you develop the powerful beliefs you need to stay focused:

Key #1—*Act from Desire for Gain, Not Fear of Loss*

Focus on what you want to have, instead of on what you don't want to lose. Give up things that relate to fear of loss. For example, don't hang on to the idea that you'll be able to live your dream with your job income if you know that's not true. Instead, do something to gain your financial freedom.

Focusing on what you want to gain, instead of what you don't want to lose, keeps your mind on positive thoughts.

This will create positive images in your subconscious and translate into positive results in your life.

Mentally let go of everything in your life that is average, especially average thinking. This will create a "vacuum," making room for the things you want. You cannot develop leadership until you let go of being a follower—*leadership is taken, not given.*

You cannot create wealth unless you let go of the habit of always being in debt. The principle of "letting go" is true for every area in your life where you want to move on. As the old saying goes, *"You can't get to second base with one foot on first."*

Key #2—*There's Plenty for Everyone*

Look at the world and everything in it with the view that there is plenty for everyone. This is a switch from the message many of us have been taught. The school system leads us to believe only a few kids can consistently excel or star in athletics. The media tries to convince us that only people with perfect bodies will enjoy a loving relationship. Our parents often instill in us the idea that "Money doesn't grow on trees," which really says there is a limited amount of it and we'd better hang on to what little we have or can get.

We also get many messages telling us that there's only so much to go around. We then start believing that by earning something for ourselves, we are depriving someone else. If we earn a lot of money for example, we must have kept someone else from earning it. The truth of the matter is, there is plenty to go around.

The "pie" we are eating from is actually getting bigger! When we enjoy our share of the pie, we never deprive anyone else of theirs. Think of it in this way. Whenever you enjoy a bite of the pie of life, that's your reward for the *contribution* you made to it. The great thing is, this just makes the pie bigger and better for everyone.

This is especially true for wealth. Wealth is really the reward earned for the expression of an idea that changes something into a more useful form. Oil is changed into gasoline. Sand is changed into silicon chips to make computers. Magnetic force is changed into electricity. Iron ore is changed into steel. Clay is fired and turned into bricks. Manufacturers turn raw materials and parts into products. This all creates multiple benefits for all of us to help each other have a better life.

Think about this for a minute: The people who discovered oil, designed computers, built automobiles, and developed franchising, network marketing and real estate empires became some of the wealthiest people on this planet. Did they take wealth away from anyone else? No. They simply helped others become wealthy, which then made *them* wealthy in the process.

What they did was *expand* the pie, giving all of us a better chance to benefit more! A much larger pie means that by creating the companies that paid them a fortune, they also created billions of dollars of additional wealth that we can all benefit from. They were the pioneers and, in the process, made a significant contribution to the world economy.

Here's another important point to remember—everything you need to create great wealth is already here. For example, all you need to do is plug into a system—the pattern of success that many have used before you—to make your dreams come true. The developers of oil wells, real estate, automobiles, and huge computer companies didn't really create anything new. All they really did was take something that already existed and changed it from one form into something more useful. And they, as well as thousands of others, made billions of dollars because of it. You too have a tremendous opportunity to expand the pie—*by focusing on your dream and making it a reality.*

Begin viewing wealth in this way. Brainstorm ideas you can use to expand the pie for everyone else. Consider how you can meet more people and develop relationships, and whatever else you can do to make it happen for you and your family. As you expand the pie for others, you will create greater wealth for yourself as well.

Key #3—*Take Responsibility for Where You Are, But Don't Let It Keep You from Where You're Going*

Don't label things. Accept where you are without labeling it as "not where you'd like to be" or "sad" or "terrible." It is the way it is because of all the choices you've made in the past, and that's okay. The only way it can be "bad" is if you decide it is. It is entirely up to you. You can also decide that it's good—or neutral—or whatever else you choose. The important thing is, you don't have to think of your current life as "awful" in order to move on to a better life. Just think positive and look for the good in your situation.

In fact, you are perfectly free to choose exactly how you want to think about anything that is occurring in your life now or has occurred in the past. Exercise your freedom in a positive manner. Choose to view everything that happens in your life as part of a great adventure. Picture yourself as always staying focused and moving along the most desirable possible path for you. Then, guess what happens when you get where you're going? You can dream even bigger!

Your life isn't a random event! Things happen for a reason. When you accept that everything happens for your own good, you'll have more peace of mind. You can then learn from your mistakes, and those of others, and move on. And sometimes you may even learn what *not* to do from others! You can then let go of considering people or things as pains or problems. Start asking yourself, "What can I learn from this situation or that person?"

And, by all means, let go of the idea that the world is out to "get" you. It's not! In fact, most of the world has no idea you even exist. The small part of the world that does is generally too caught up in its own circumstances to care much about getting you. The people you think are thinking about you probably aren't! They're probably too busy thinking about themselves and their own challenges to be concerned about you.

I would recommend adopting one of two viewpoints:

One, quit labeling events. Just accept them as they are and move on, without judging them as good or bad.

Or two, acknowledge it is challenging to live in a modern, complex society—but don't make any judgments. Just choose to have a positive attitude. Every challenge or setback is simply an opportunity for you to grow and become.

Key #4—*Do What You Can Do, and Don't Worry about the Rest*

The final key to developing a powerful belief system is to choose beliefs and options that *you*, personally, can do something about. Of course, it's even better to have people doing things in cooperation with you.

It is your responsibility to be the best person *you* can be and serve as a positive example to others. It is not your responsibility to change the world, or even one other person in it. You can't change anyone else. But, you can make a difference in the world by contributing the best way you know how. You can positively affect others by having a cheerful attitude and setting a good example for them.

Get a clean sheet of paper and write down, across the top of the page, the five categories of: 1) spiritual or religious; 2) personal and business relationships, including family; 3) money and finances; 4) career and business; and 5) health and exercise. Under each one, write down what kinds of beliefs you need to adopt in order to live your dream and fulfill your mission. While you are doing this, keep the four keys to developing powerful beliefs, which we just discussed, in the back of your mind.

Now ask yourself these questions:

♦ What beliefs would a person who is living my dream hold?
♦ What beliefs would a person who is fulfilling a mission like mine hold?
♦ What beliefs would allow me to enjoy the most happiness without conflicting with my values?

Stay Focused by Choosing Direct Alternatives

Direct alternatives are those in which *you personally take action until you get the results you want.* Indirect alternatives are when you *influence* the attitudes of others with the hope they will do what you want.

For example, suppose you feel your taxes are too high. An indirect alternative would be to spend hundreds of hours running a campaign to lower them. A direct alternative would be to invest your time in earning more money so you still have plenty left after paying taxes. You could also minimize them by taking advantage of any deduction and tax shelters, which are legally available to you.

Suppose you work for a boss you don't like. You might think an indirect alternative would be to attempt changing your boss. But that doesn't work. You can't change anyone but yourself. This alternative would probably be temporary at best. If you really like your job, you could have a heart to heart talk with your boss, to air your differences and discuss how you could make the situation better! A direct alternative would be to find a job with a boss you like, or start your own business. Doing this would give you the opportunity to *be* the boss, and therefore have more control over your situation.

Imagine you are a salesperson who wants to sell ten widgets a day to provide a nice income for your family. An indirect alternative would be to spend time trying to convince everyone on the street that they need your widgets. A direct alternative would be to find people whose self-interest would be satisfied by your widget. Show them clearly how they would be served by purchasing your widget.

When you are assessing a situation ask yourself, "Is there something I can do about it and is this what I want for myself? Does it fit with my values, mission and focus?" If you answered yes, then great. However, if you answered no, then calmly look elsewhere for a situation that better meets your long-term needs. Now that you understand the importance of direct alternatives, you need to find out what may be holding you back from taking them.

Most people's lives can be compared to a man-carrying helium balloon straining against its ground anchoring ropes. As soon as the ropes are released, it rises smoothly and effortlessly into the sky. When more altitude is needed, the pilot simply throws out sandbags and the decrease in weight allows it to continue its climb.

You're the same way. Your natural state is to soar high in the sky, like a helium balloon. But you may be holding yourself back by keeping your balloon anchored to the ground or not releasing your sandbags. Before you can throw out all the sandbags in your life, you need to be aware of them Then, you can develop a strategy to eliminate them so you can soar into the clear blue sky. Begin by examining your overall views of the world, commonly called your paradigm, frame of reference, or beliefs.

Chapter 6

Let Go Of Your Limiting Beliefs

"All that a man does outwardly is but the expression and completion of his inward thought. To work effectively, he must think clearly; to act nobly, he must think nobly."
William Ellerly Channing

Get Rid of Your *"Excess Baggage"*

One of the reasons it may have been difficult for you to stay focused is that you were dragging around some *"excess baggage."* It would be in the form of beliefs that aren't appropriate for the dream you're endeavoring to live.

When people first hear this at my seminars or during personal coaching, they often challenge me. After all, they tell me, "My beliefs are 'common sense' and I know they're right or I wouldn't believe them."

"If your beliefs are so correct," I always ask, "then how come your life isn't as you'd like it to be?" That usually gets them thinking a bit. Then I ask them to recall the story of Christopher Columbus.

Before Columbus sailed, it was "common sense" wisdom that the world was flat. Everyone "knew" that was true and people behaved accordingly. Old Chris, however, decided this paradigm was flawed. He decided to adopt a new belief, or frame of reference.

His belief of the world not being flat led him to ask, "How can I sail *around* the world?" instead of "How far can I go before I fall off the end of the earth?"

He formed an image in his mind of himself sailing successfully around the world, discovering new trade routes and trading partners. He became emotionally involved with this idea and would not give up on it.

Despite the ridicule he received from his "educated" peers who "knew" he was wrong, Columbus persisted. Finally, he convinced Queen Isabella of Spain to outfit his ships and, as they say, the rest is history.

Columbus' successful voyage changed the beliefs of people around the world. So we now act under a frame of reference that knows the world is round.

You can make dramatic changes everyday and become *naturally focused* in your own life, simply by changing the beliefs you work under. Before you can successfully do this, however, you need to understand something. The "common sense" beliefs you may have adopted are probably preventing you from staying focused on achieving your dreams and goals.

The Six Limiting Beliefs That Keep Most People from Being Focused

Limiting Belief #1—*"I Can't Do It"*
Many of you are holding yourself back by believing others have innate talents and abilities that you don't, and could never develop. This is simply not true. We were all created equal—with the opportunity to excel and become unequal by developing and using our skills and talents.

Yes, it is true that some of us are born with certain physical and mental tendencies that seem to give us an advantage in certain areas. However, in many cases, others can "level the playing field" by using the laws of goal achievement. They can *develop* a set of talents that will enable them to function just as well as the "natural."

One of the best examples of this is the Wright Brothers, inventors of the airplane. They were not blessed with the natural talent of flying. In fact, no one was! But they got inspired by the idea and decided that's what they wanted to do. They put thoughts into their conscious minds. Every day they built images of themselves flying free as the birds. They got emotionally involved with these ideas and it became second nature for them to take the necessary actions. They overcame all kinds of obstacles and ridicule along the way, and almost lost their lives doing it. They observed the birds, studied what had been already done, and designed and built their gliders based on their findings and beliefs. They kept redesigning and building until they got the answers they were looking for.

The result? Orville and Wilbur Wright, bicycle mechanics that didn't even go to college, accomplished what no other man, since the beginning of time, was able to do. They gave mankind the airplane, one of the world's greatest inventions, and two entire industries—aerospace and the airlines!

Next time you find yourself thinking, "Gee, I'd sure like to do that, but I can't," ask yourself...

- ♦ Why do I believe I can't?
- ♦ Is there a rational reason for my belief?
- ♦ Could I be mistaken in my belief?
- ♦ Then ask, "How *can* I accomplish this?

Make a list of possible ways you *could* accomplish your goals, even if most of them seem outrageous or "impossible" at this time. What you will find, in most situations, is that by shifting your paradigm to "There is a way," you will actually find it! Someone once said, *"Knock the 't' off can't. 'Can't' will lose its power and turn into 'can.'"*

Limiting Belief #2—*"Things Need Fixing"*

Ninety-nine percent of the things you think need fixing are fine just the way they are. All they may need is to be understood, not fixed. When you understand how they really work you'll realize that, most often, they're not broken. What may need fixing is your perception of the situation, not the situation itself.

Approach everything like an experimental scientist. In your relationships, first get a good understanding of the other person and their set of beliefs, values, and the way they look at the world. Then, work together to understand how both of you would like the relationship to work. Both of you need to build this image of an ideal relationship in your minds and turn it over to your subconscious so it can help you to create it in physical reality.

Limiting Belief #3—*"I See Things the Right Way"*

This is the belief that says the way you see things *now* is the only way to see things or, at least, it's the right way to see them.

Any physicist will tell you that matter and energy are continuously changing. Matter is constantly being converted into energy and energy is constantly being changed into matter. This is shown in a basic way by Einstein's famous equation, $E=Mc^2$. This says that energy equals mass times the speed of light squared. According to this equation, energy and mass are related.

Since energy and mass are constantly changing, and everything we see is made up of them, the entire world around us is constantly changing. The only thing we can say for sure is that, "This is how I perceive things." We cannot say for certain, "This is how it is," for two reasons.

First, since everything is constantly changing, by the time we finish saying something, things will have changed. Second, the way we think things are is determined by our past experiences, which affects what we "see" in our world today. Even two relatively similar people, like twins, can have totally different perceptions of the exact same thing.

For example, let's say you and your best friend go to the forest and look at the trees. You might remember your first kiss in the soft sunlight filtering between the branches of the trees. You probably think the forest is friendly and inviting. Your friend, however, might remember how he got lost in the forest when he was a little kid and didn't think he'd ever see his mommy again. To him, the forest may look frightening and uninviting.

Same forest. Same time. Totally different perception. And both perceptions are "right" for the person doing the perceiving.

There is no right or wrong when it comes to beauty, either. It, too, is based on perception. As the old saying goes, *"Beauty is in the eye of the beholder."* Also, *"One man's junk is another man's treasure."* No one views everything in the exact same way.

If you looked at a television screen under a microscope, you would see thousands of flashing dots in all kinds of different colors. The changes in colors would look very random to you. After a while, all their flashing and color changing might even begin to irritate you. If, however, you took a few steps back and looked at the same screen from three or four feet away, you might see a beautiful sunset on a lush tropical island. Same picture. Different perception. Both are real. Both are right.

Your perception of the world is only partially correct. If it works for you, fine. But, don't try to force it onto others; it may not work the same for them. And, keep an open mind so you're always looking to understand the parts of "reality" you currently do not perceive. As Henry David Thoreau once said in *Walden*...

"...If men would steadily observe realities only, and not allow themselves to be deluded, life...would be like a fairy

tale...we perceive that only great and worthy things have any permanent and absolute existence...Men establish and confirm their daily life of routine and habit everywhere, which still is built on purely illusory foundations. Children, who play life, discern its true law..."

Remember, you presently "see" and perceive the world based on *your* experiences, beliefs, and the way you are. In essence, *your world* is a reflection of you. By raising your level of awareness and broadening your perspective, you will better understand how things really are. As you gain more focus, you will experience a new, more productive and enriching level of life.

Limiting Belief #4—*"It's Not My Fault"*

How many times have you heard this one? "I'm not responsible for that." "I couldn't help it." "Things like that just happen." "It's not my fault."

These are just excuses! Things don't just happen. You *can* help it, and you need to take responsibility for it. And by this time, you probably know exactly why. You either choose the thoughts that enter your conscious mind or allow information, such as TV programs, to seep in. This information forms images in your subconscious which dutifully goes to work to turn them into physical reality. It triggers a set of emotions that cause your actions, which in turn create results, which lead to your success or failure.

You *are* responsible for every single result in your life—*all* of them. Period. It's up to you. Take responsibility, take charge, and get the results you want.

One of the most common areas where people attempt to brush off their own responsibility is in the area of wealth and money. Have you ever heard someone who's a little (or a lot) short on cash say something like: "It's not my fault. They laid me off," or "The economy stinks. No one can make money in an economy like this," or "I grew up poor and never had a chance," or "There's virtue in poverty"? Have *you* ever said or thought any of these things?

All of these are examples of people trying to avoid responsibility to justify the results in their lives. Let's go ahead and de-bunk these myths right now.

If you got laid off, you may not have been contributing enough to the company to justify your pay. It's also possible that the company heads, for whatever reason, didn't see your contribution. Or maybe the company was taken over, downsized, or its sales dropped. Whatever the case may be, no one owes you a living. Why do you think it's called earning a living and not getting a living?

If you aren't contributing more than what someone is paying you, don't expect to keep getting a check. In fact, if you aren't contributing perhaps ten times what they're paying you for, you'll probably be looking for work soon. There are plenty of eager people out there who would be happy to contribute that much to get your pay.

If the company heads are not as competent as they could be, and didn't realize your contribution, or sales have dropped, you probably don't want to work for them. It's not a wise use of your time to spend your hours working for someone who doesn't appreciate your value or isn't taking care of business. You may want to find a job elsewhere.

If you are really as good as you think you are, other companies will realize this and want to hire you. If they don't, maybe you need to re-think how good you really are. Maybe you need to go out and improve your knowledge level and skills so you are more valuable in the marketplace.

Remember, if you're building your own business on the side, you need to have a steady income until you build it big and secure enough to walk away from your job. In the meantime, keep learning and growing yourself, so you can be your personal best in all areas of your life. This will help you be the best employee you can be...while you're working your job.

People tell me all the time, "Well, I really want to work for *that* particular company," or "I don't want to move my family to take a new job elsewhere." That's fine, but don't complain if you lose your job. You just made the decision that you value working for *that* particular company or staying in *this* particular geographic location, more than going out and taking advantage of a different opportunity.

There's nothing wrong with your preferences. Just be prepared to face the consequences, because it's a choice *you* are making. Fortunately, it's also a choice you're free to change at any moment. And remember, we live in a world of unprecedented opportunity.

The "bottom line" is, take responsibility for everything in your life and you'll be on your way to being more successful. Remember, it's not what happens to you that matters; it's how you respond to it that makes the difference.

Limiting Belief #5—*"Others Should Do Things Exactly the Way I Would"*

This one leads people astray all the time, too. Others don't have to, and probably will not, do things exactly the way you would, so don't expect them to.

We are all unique. Each of us is the product of a different set of habits, beliefs, conditioning and experiences. Our subconscious sorts out information in a different manner. Our feelings and emotions are different. We all perceive the world in a slightly different way. To expect others to act in the same way as we would in a given situation is sheer folly.

Each time you expect someone else to act in a certain way, you are probably setting yourself up for disappointment. If they don't see the situation the same way you do, they will not have the same feeling about it. It's highly unlikely they would act the exact same way you would. If you expect them to, you'll be disappointed virtually every time.

Trying to put others into a "box" that is just like yours is also a form of prejudice and is controlling. It's simply pre-judging someone before you know all the facts, and forcing your will on them. If you expect someone to behave as you would, you are denying that person's individuality. You are pre-judging the way you think they'll behave, without knowing all the facts about their particular situation.

We all have gifts and talents to offer the world through our unique personalities. And, after all, nobody *has* to do anything! It's all a choice. If you keep telling people what they *should* be doing, you'll soon alienate them and drive them away! Instead, tell them what they *could* do if they want certain results.

Eliminate your expectations about others' behavior and practice acceptance instead. Accept them for who they are. Don't try to change them, because you can't! Instead, set a good example for them to follow. When they want to grow, they'll change in response to your leadership.

This sends the message that you truly care about them as an individual. *Accept them as they are, but look at them as they can be.* Believe in everyone, but count on no one.

Limiting Belief #6—*"I've Already Spent Too Much Time Doing This Without Getting the Results I Wanted"*

Many people believe that the time, effort, and money they've spent in the past in striving for certain goals must be considered when making a decision in the present—especially if what they've already done hasn't given them their desired results. But this is probably because they quit too soon, and didn't develop themselves personally so they could get the results they wanted. The truth is, you are not tied to a past failure unless *you* bind yourself to it. And you're the only one who can do that to yourself.

The only thing you have today is the present value of an investment. Ask yourself, "How can I make the most of this in the present and the future?" Here are a few examples for you to consider:

Some individual stock market investors who lose money do so because they are caught up in this trap. They sell winner stocks too soon, then rationalize their decision by saying, "I just got tired of the ups and downs." They seem to forget that historically the stock market has grown over 10 percent annually. By not "hanging in there" for the long term they spoil the potential of making the kind of money they otherwise could.

What every successful stock market investor needs to continually ask is, "What is the best use of my money today? What is the best investment I can make with these dollars today?" Make sure you know what a sound investment is. And don't start randomly buying and selling stocks because you see "greener pastures" somewhere else. Get advice from a successful broker you know, like and trust, and let them help you manage your portfolio. Then pick a winner and stay with it.

The amount of money you originally invested is basically irrelevant. The only thing you have today is the current value of the investment, so it doesn't matter how much you paid for it. All that matters is whether or not that investment has bright prospects for making you money in the future. If it does, hold on. If it doesn't, sell it immediately and move on to something else with more potential.

What if you're not yet in the financial position to even consider stocks? In that case, invest time and money in yourself, which is actually your best investment. You need to first grow yourself before you can grow your bank account. Then, once you're out of debt and have excess money, you'll be in a better position to look at various financial vehicles in which you could invest!

What About "Holding On" to Certain "Friendships"?

Countless people rationalize their dead-end friendships thinking, "I've got to make this work. I've invested too much time and energy in this to let it go now." Maybe you think this is true for the circle of friends you had before you decided to move on and improve your life. It's simply unrealistic to think all your friends will want to move on just because you do. Everyone has their own life to live.

The time and energy you've invested in friendships in the past is totally irrelevant to how successful those relationships are today or could be tomorrow. Are you still close to your elementary school, high school, or even college friends? Probably not. As we go through life, our friendships and associations change. Granted, some may be with us for life, but most won't. If you don't do a lot of things together with someone, the bond weakens and that's okay.

It is impossible for you to live in the past, but that's what "holding on" is causing you to mentally do. The only place you can ever live is the present. Don't spend time and energy holding on to the past. Let go *now* and get on with your life.

Ask yourself, "Is this friendship one that I want today? Do I feel healthy, vibrant, and positive about this relationship and the other person involved in it?" If the answer is "yes," great. Enjoy every single moment of your wonderful friendship. If the answer is no, move on. There's no reason to spend time holding on to "friendships" that don't work anymore, just because you think you've invested too much time to let them go.

Some people believe that if they let someone go, especially if they were once a best friend, they'll be lonely and won't ever find anyone else to fill the void. If you have ever thought that, remember two things.

First, you don't need any one particular person in your life. Relationships certainly enhance life, but they don't totally define it. You can probably do just fine without that person, especially if they're negative-thinking and trying to steal your dream. Anyone who would do that could hardly be considered your friend. A true friend would encourage you, and not be negative or try to hold you back.

Second, the only time you could probably be lonely is when you are insecure and don't know yourself. Once you know who you really are and where you're going, you won't ever feel lonely again. You will have such a rich life that it won't bother you one iota to give up an unhealthy relationship. That would be like a good spring-cleaning. It makes room for new, healthier relationships to come into your life. Surround yourself with positive-thinking people who are excited about life and going somewhere.

And, by all means, don't persecute yourself for relationships that didn't work. Every time you dwell on them, you're missing the beauty of the present moment; you're living in the past. Remember, each moment comes only once in your life and you can end up missing an awful lot of them if you're not careful. Let go of the past. Don't judge it as good or bad. Don't dwell on it. It just was and it's over. You lived, you learned, and you're moving on. As successful businesspeople often say, *"don't throw good money after bad."*

The time, energy, and money you have invested in something in the past doesn't have to influence you when it comes to making new decisions in the present. Make your decisions from the "clean slate" of the present moment. Don't cloud them by hanging onto the past. The past is gone and you can't do anything about it, so let it go. View each moment as a blank page. Decide exactly what's best for you. What will contribute most to living your dream in line with your mission and values, and doing the right thing? Then do it, joyously and without hesitation.

Chapter 7

Think Like The Wealthy!

"You are what you think about all day long."
Ralph Waldo Emerson

What Are Your Beliefs About Money?

Are you as wealthy as you would like to be? Most people aren't because they have false beliefs about money that hold them back from creating all the prosperity they could have. Understanding what money is, how it works, and what it is and isn't good for, allows you to create a new wealth paradigm. This may sound elementary, but it's an essential part of financially moving on.

First of all, "what is money?" It's a symbol of value and a medium of exchange. It is a convenient way to trade goods and services. I'm sure you find it more convenient to carry money than a sack full of products. I'm sure Lee Iacocca, the former CEO of Chrysler Corporation, would say the same thing about carrying around a trailer full of cars. Money represents the value we place on various goods and services. Since it is a symbol, it has no value in and of itself. Its only value is that which we assign to it.

You can view money as the reward you receive for services rendered and products sold. It's similar to receiving a plaque for being "employee of the month." The difference is, when you receive money, you can exchange it for other things you want and need instead of just hanging it on a wall! If you want more money, serve more people.

Keeping the role of money in perspective will help free you from any negative thoughts you may have about wealth. Earn money joyously and never feel guilty about it. At the same time, don't let money rule your life either. Ironically, it's usually those who don't have much money who let it rule their lives. Once you have "the money problem" solved, you'll be deciding what to do with your *extra* money!

Take to heart the words of American showman and author, P.T. Barnum—*"Money is a terrible master, but an excellent servant."* Think of money as a servant that follows your every command. It's up to you, as its master, to take responsibility for giving it orders to do good. Once money is no longer an issue in your life, you are freed up to do more good than you've ever imagined.

Now, let's go on to the five false beliefs about money. They need to be eliminated for you to stay on track and focused so you can achieve the wealth you desire.

False Money Belief #1—*"I Want or Need Money."*

The truth is, you *don't* really want or need money! "What?" you say! Well, think about it for a minute. What you really want or need is what you can *do* with it.

Imagine being hungry. Say you can't eat because you don't have any money. You're walking dejectedly down the street when, out-of-the-blue, a stranger appears and offers you a million dollars. Your eyes light up and you follow him to where the money is located. He ushers you into a room full of cash, piled high with wads of currency.

You're ecstatic until you hear the door shut and lock behind you. You look around and realize you now have more money than you could have ever imagined. But you still can't eat. You're locked in a room with no food. You now realize what you really wanted was food, not money.

Keep this in mind as you go through your day. You really want *what money can buy*—not the money itself.

Money is a convenient medium of exchange used to get the things you want, but it is not the only way to do it. You could directly trade some products or services for what you want. And you would be just as satisfied as if you bought it with money, wouldn't you?

Don't get caught up in just "making" money. You can't really want the money anyway. Money is only a symbol—a tool. It has no intrinsic value. What you really want or need is what you can do with it. Money gives you *options*.

False Money Belief #2—*"It Takes Money to Make Money"*

This is not totally true. There are actually two basic ways to make money—people at work and money at work. If you don't have money to put to work, you can always put people to work—yourself and others.

The key that unlocks wealth's power of multiplication is *ideas* that can be duplicated. The only thing it really takes to make money is a good idea that can be duplicated by others. And the idea doesn't even have to be yours! The Burger King and Hardee's franchises were not new ideas. They were just "copycats," or duplicators, of a concept that McDonald's pioneered and proved successful. Similarly, network marketing was also pioneered and proved successful back in the 1950s and is now being duplicated by millions.

Remember these key points:

1. First, there is always a way. Every time you have a desire it is a sign of an unfulfilled potential inside you. You do not get true desires that cannot be fulfilled. So, if you truly desire to be wealthy, you can do it. The way already exists. You need to be aware of it and do whatever it takes to make it happen.

2. Second, remember, all you need is one good idea acted upon and you could be set for life. Bill Gates of Microsoft, Rich DeVos and Jay Van Andel of Amway, Tom Monaghan of Domino's Pizza fame, and Ray Kroc, king of McDonald's golden arches, all had one good idea that they acted upon. In the process, they attracted other people who wanted to work with them and share in their success. This, along with action, determination, patience, and a positive attitude, was basically all it took to make them some of the wealthiest people in the world! And that's all it will take for you to become financially independent for life...even if you're starting today with no money.

3. Third, your opportunity to create wealth is right in your own "backyard." The way for us to become wealthy is usually right under our noses. We just need to open our eyes and our minds to the possibilities.

In Russell Cronwell's famous speech, "Acres of Diamonds," he tells the true story of an old Persian farmer named Al Hafed. After years of searching around the world for the riches he so desired, it was found that Al Hafed's own backyard contained one of the world's richest diamond mines—after he had sold the property!

Remember your acres of diamonds. How about all the people you know and could meet who could become part of your dream. You probably already know a lot of people and could meet a lot more. You could become wealthy by "mining" or prospecting them, building a relationship and sharing your opportunity or idea with them.

False Money Belief #3—"I'm Not Smart Enough to Become Wealthy"

That's simply not true. Many of the wealthiest people in the world never even finished school. And, in fact, some of the most "educated" people in the world, many who might have more than one degree, are barely making ends meet.

The truth is, it doesn't take great brains to become wealthy. All it takes is one simple idea acted upon and stuck with until we make it work for ourselves.

Think about it. Did it take a rocket scientist to produce a hamburger, pizza, a pair of jeans, or a bar of soap? Hardly. Yet, Ray Kroc, Tom Monaghan, Levi Strauss, and Proctor and Gamble all became rich and famous for figuring out what to do with these simple products. The greatest minds usually think of the simplest things, then act on them. The most successful people are those who see some simple need and then fill it. They understand that when they find a need for something, there are other people out there who need it too.

The only thing you need to do to become wealthy is find out what people want, not just need, and then share it with them. It's that simple. You don't have to beat your head against the wall trying to come up with some new, high-tech gadget or whizbang invention. Just think of the *"KISS"* principle—*Keep It Simple Sweetheart!*

Look around you every day and you will see all kinds of people with wants you could fill. That's what the inventors of Leggs pantyhose did. The founders of the great motel chains realized weary travelers wanted safe, clean places to sleep. The original fast food kings realized that the accelerating pace of most everyone's lives meant we would be eating out more often than ever before.

Pick a need that gets you excited and figure out a way to fill it. You can do that no matter what your supposed IQ or educational level may be, so get started today. In general, simply help enough other people get what they want, and you'll get what you want.

False Money Belief #4—*"Money Is the Root of All Evil"*

Here's one of the common myths that holds people back from ever achieving financial security. How many times have you heard people tell you that the Bible says money is the root of all evil? Anyone who believes that, needs to go back and take another look at their Bible.

What the Bible really says is, "The love of money is a root of evil." Money itself isn't evil. Get some money out of your wallet right now and look at it closely. Is there anything about it that looks evil to you? Can you find anything evil about a piece of paper with some ink on it? It's not the money itself that's evil. It's what a person does with it that could be evil. Money is just a tool; a medium of exchange. When used properly, money is a faithful servant that will enable you to do all kinds of good in the world. You can have all the good intentions in the world, but if there isn't money behind them, it may be difficult to accomplish many of your goals—no matter how altruistic they may be.

Have you ever heard the biblical story of the Good Samaritan? He would never have been remembered for just good intentions. Here's how it goes: A Jewish man was traveling on the dangerous road from Jerusalem to Jericho when thieves jumped him, beat him and left him for dead. Soon, a man came by and saw the injured man, but ignored him and went on his way. A little later, another man came along, but he, too, ignored the victim. Finally, a Samaritan, who normally avoided this road, discovered the man in distress. He not only stopped to comfort him, but also carried him to an inn. He then paid the innkeeper two days' wages to cover the man's needs for rest and recovery. For that he is remembered and revered 2000 years later. But he couldn't have done it without money!

The same is true for religious leaders. Without money, they could not build churches. Nor could they operate programs to help the homeless, the spiritually, mentally and physically challenged, and others who need support.

Without money, we could not feed starving children in Third World nations or build schools and hospitals. Without money, we would have no museums and orchestras to enjoy.

Not to mention that, without money, we would probably have no clothes on our backs, no roofs over our heads, no cars to drive, no food to eat, and no warm beds to sleep in. Money is the only thing that can be used to do what it does. And the more of it you have, the more good you can do with it, and the more options you have.

As for me, I've chosen the prosperity in my life—along with the clothing, shelter, food, bed and opportunity to help others—that money brings. And you can choose the prosperous life as well. Eliminate the idea that money is evil. Begin telling yourself that *"Money is my friend. It is an obedient servant that will do whatever I ask of it. And, as a benevolent and moral master, I will only ask money to perform duties that benefit myself and others."* That is a prosperous, healthy attitude about money. Cultivate this attitude by always asking yourself, "What good things will I do with the money I am making? How will this money help me and others lead happier, more fulfilling lives?"

False Money Belief #5—*"Making More Money Will Solve All My Problems"*

If you think money will solve all your problems, think again. Challenges are a part of life, and you're going to have them as long as you live. The truth about challenges is they can't be solved on the same level as they occur. The way to resolve a situation is to mentally raise yourself to a level above it. It either resolves itself because it was only temporary (you had patience), you change your attitude about it, or you become aware of the solution. During the process, you grew and became more than you were.

Just throwing money itself at problems never solves them! It may slow them down in the short term, but that's about it. You need to get to the cause. Imagine your problem as a cut on your hand that needs stitches. You place a bandage over it, which seems to solve the problem, but all it is doing is temporarily covering it up. It is doing nothing for healing the real cause of the problem. The real solution is to get the wound properly cleaned, disinfected, stitched and then bandaged.

Now, if the *creative* solution to a problem includes spending money, then it's a part of the solution. For example, say you've set a business or professional goal to reach by the end of the year. The problem is, you have some responsibilities at home. If you have children old enough, you could give them chores to do in a spirit of teamwork. Let them know they'd be working *with* mom and dad to give everyone a better life. If your kids are too young, or already grown, perhaps you could hire someone to help you. They could clean the house, mow the lawn, weed your flowerbeds, and baby-sit your children—while you and your spouse invest time in building your business or profession.

Some people say that if a problem can be solved with money, it's really not a problem at all, just a situation. Then you might say—*there are no problems, only solutions!*

In the case of needing to delegate some responsibilities, the situation may be that you have yet to realize how valuable your time is. Your challenge, therefore, is to put more value on your time. Then parting with the money to pay the help makes sense. Look at it this way, if you're hiring a high school or college student to do a chore, you're contributing to their being able to put gas in their car, buy clothes, or something else they need. You're boosting the economy and helping secure the future. You're also freeing up your time to do what you need to do to pursue your dream.

Since the real source of all your problems is in your attitude or thinking, you can also solve them by choosing to either react or respond. Whatever happens to you is not nearly as important to your success as how you respond to it! For example, if you just react to a situation, you may express the first emotion you feel, like anger, and jump to conclusions without thinking it through. Whereas, when you respond, you do your best to put yourself "in the other persons' shoes" and understand the challenge from both sides.

This applies to every situation you face in your life. You are always free to respond to a situation, rather than just react, in any way you choose. You can also decide whether to perceive the situation as good or bad. And you can change your conditioning so that your desired responses become natural, like your reactions used to be.

The conditioning that determines how you naturally react or respond to a situation, as well as the thoughts you use to change that conditioning, originates in your mind. It is really inside your own mind that your problems start. So you need to question your thinking about the challenge first.

To truly solve a problem, long-term, you need to "rise above it." Since your mind functions on the higher, intellectual level, you need to resolve your situations there. Think them through to come up with appropriate responses. Throwing money at a problem, which is a reaction, is like trying to solve the problem on the lower, physical level. It cannot be done successfully on a permanent basis. To change your results, you need to change your thinking.

Most people misunderstand this. When they have inner feelings of insecurity or low self-esteem, they may go out and buy new clothes or cars or other "toys," in an attempt to replace their feelings of emptiness. This is why so many so-called rich people are unhappy. They scrambled their entire lives to make money, thinking that would solve all their problems. Then, when they got the money and it didn't solve a single problem, they ran out and spent more, thinking, "Maybe this'll do it." And, of course, it doesn't.

Many people stand in unemployment lines because they're not educated enough to find a decent job or because their conditioning prevents them from holding a permanent one. The unemployment office gives them money until they get a job, which they may hold for a couple of weeks. Soon, they are back in the unemployment line. What happened? Their problem is mental or emotional while the helping agencies are trying to solve it on a physical level. It just doesn't work. This person may need help with their knowledge and skill, attitude, self-confidence, and self-esteem.

If you don't have enough money to pay your bills, you may be tempted to blame your employer for not paying you enough, or the slow economy for preventing you from getting a job. You may think more money will solve the problem. It won't. It will just temporarily cover it up. Unless you change what's in your mind and heart, the problem will occur again. Your challenges "live" in your own mind and heart. When we are aware of the characteristics we need to develop in order to become successful, like vision—focused and determined—we can excel in almost any arena. When we are aware of what businesses and professions thrive, even in a down economy, we can invest our energy in that direction.

No matter what laws are passed or what shape the economy is in, some people make money while others lose it. Why? Those who are truly wealthy understand money is a medium of exchange. They understand the laws governing the creation of wealth and follow them. They don't use money as a bandage for their problems.

Don't turn to money as the cure for all your problems, and don't blame the lack of money as the cause of all your problems. If you have either of these attitudes, you will never become truly wealthy. Instead, realize that *money is a reward for ideas and products shared or services rendered.* If you want more money, simply serve more people in a deeper, more beneficial manner.

Address your problems at their source—your mind. Raise your awareness so you realize that either your problems will dissipate or you find simple, natural solutions to them. You could start doing this by asking, "What's right about this situation? How could I respond more positively? What would I be feeling if I was the other person? What unskillful behavior am I responsible for? Will my negative reaction actually improve the situation or will it just cause me stress?" Don't react to the situation. Just stay neutral and observe it.

Since your reactions come entirely from your own mind, you are perfectly free to choose *not* to react. You can choose to *respond* compassionately with self-responsibility. Tell yourself, "I am choosing not to react to this situation. I realize the situation is not negative unless I view it so, and I am choosing to look for the good in it. I am observing what is happening without reacting. I am sorting it out. Looking at both sides. Then, if necessary, with kindness, I'll share how I feel about the behavior, rather than the person."

Experiment with that attitude. It will pay big dividends. Soon you will be liberating the mental energy you have had tied up in reacting negatively to various situations.

You'll be able to reinvest all this extra energy into creating positive, mutually beneficial relationships and growing stronger as you generate trust and mutual respect. That's a wonderful reward for not reacting negatively to the situations around you, and having compassion for others.

Chapter 8

The "Magic" Of Goal-Achievement

"Destiny is not a matter of chance, it is a matter of choice; it is not a thing to be waited for, it is a thing to be achieved."
William Jennings Bryan

Goal-Achievement Is a Process

We are now ready to move on to the good stuff—setting and achieving goals that will enable you to live your dream. Using the principles of goal-achievement, you can stay calm and focused more than ever before. In the next few chapters, you will learn a process that has helped people turn their dreams into reality. And, it can do the same for you. Follow each step, in order, and don't skip anything or shortcut the system. Remember, goal-achievement is a process that works only when you work it.

Do You Have Goals?

Studies have found that 97 percent of people never set any goals at all. They just drift through life without any real direction—like a ship without a rudder. The 3 percent of people who do set goals accomplish more than the other 97 percent combined!

Unfortunately, most people spend more time planning a party than they do their lives. They spend more time in front of the television than all the time they invest in setting and achieving goals during their entire lifetime. The results of this lack of concern for realizing our potential and expressing our talents are even sadder. According to the U.S. Dept. of Labor, only five percent of Americans are financially independent by age 65. The other 95 depend on friends and relatives, and their monthly Social Security checks, just to survive. (If you don't live in the U.S., you may have different statistics, but the situation may be similar.)

We cannot blame this statistic on lack of income or job opportunity, either. Even in the high-income professions such as medicine and law, only five out of every hundred people are financially free at age 65. And that's after 40 years of earning some of the highest incomes in the country.

What's the problem here? Obviously, most people don't manage their money or activities very well. Just as important, though, most have no *plan* for doing so. In most cases, it's simply the lack of a simple, doable plan that holds most people back from achieving the financial prosperity and other goals they would like to achieve.

The same holds true for the rest of our lives. No one would build a house without a blueprint, but most people try to build a successful life without a plan. Trying just doesn't make it so. *Planning* and *doing* is the answer.

In this chapter you will begin to understand, or perhaps be reminded, what goals really are, why they're important, and how the goal-achievement process works. Then you'll learn exactly how to choose appropriate goals and how to develop a plan to achieve them. When you follow this process, you can be one of the "five-percenters" who achieve their goals and live their dream. That's exciting, isn't it?

What Is a Goal?

Before you can begin setting and achieving your goals, you need to know what a goal really is. Take a minute and finish this sentence: "To me, a goal is..."

If you completed the sentence with something like, "A goal is something I need," you're a bit off-track. If you completed the sentence with something like, "A goal is something I want," congratulations. You have an excellent understanding of what goals really are.

Goals are *wants*, not needs, with a deadline. They bridge the gap between where you are today and where you *want* to be in the tomorrows of your life. And the greater your wants, the more important your goals become.

Why Are Goals Important?

Goals are important because of the person you become in the process of achieving them! A great goal gives you the incentive to grow in awareness—an awareness of your own inherent potential, and of the beauty and joy in the world around you. A great goal also makes you aware of how you can use your knowledge and skills to create a better world for yourself and those you care about.

Don't get caught-up in running after goals just to check them off your list, while forgetting about the person you need to become in the process. You may achieve some of your goals but you will do so with a gnawing emptiness inside.

Remember these key points:

♦ You need to become more in order to achieve more.
♦ What you become determines what you achieve.
♦ What you become is more important than what you do.
♦ The real reason to set and achieve goals is for growth.

Every aspect of your life, both inner and outer, is a direct reflection of your level of awareness. You cannot be, do, have or enjoy anything until you first become aware of it.

If you didn't know there was a baseball game down the street, you couldn't enjoy the summer sun warming your arms as you munched on a hot dog from your bleacher seat. If you weren't aware of your potential to earn $100,000 or more, you would never even set a goal to attempt it. If you weren't in love with your spouse, would you have married them? If you weren't aware of all the wonderful things they've done for you, how could you appreciate and compliment them?

It's impossible for you to be, do, have or enjoy anything new until you become aware of it. However, it *is* possible for you to be, do, have, or enjoy *anything* new *once you become aware of it*. This is the real benefit of goal-setting.

When you focus on a goal, you immediately begin improving because you have become aware of a new and exciting direction to take your life in! You're already mentally shifting in that direction. You're changing your focus, which is necessary before you're able to take appropriate action and create your new reality. As you progress toward achieving your goal, your life continues to improve. As you take each step along the way you're increasing your level of awareness.

That's why it's so critically important that you set and achieve goals that are meaningful to *you*. Goals give *you* a reason to continually raise your level of awareness and grow as a human being. There are many benefits to doing this, including what you're contributing to the world, as well as a richer life experience for yourself. Everyone wins!

As your level of awareness increases, your life improves naturally and seemingly effortlessly. Untold possibilities for creative expression and beautiful appreciation will unfold.

The True Purpose of Goals

As author, entrepreneur, and speaker, Jim Rohn says, *"The true purpose of goals is to compel you to become the person it takes to achieve them."* So start increasing your level of awareness and setting some extraordinary goals so you can grow and become the best person you can be.

Chapter 9

The Laws Of Focus

"The reasonable man adapts himself to the world; the unreasonable one persists in trying to adapt the world to himself."
George Bernard Shaw

Stay On Track and Focused Every Day

Staying focused on achieving your goals works the same way as all the other processes in your life—according to an unchanging set of fundamental laws.

The first step in goal-achievement is to understand these laws and principles so you can put their incredible power to work for you. Here they are:

Focus Law #1—*You Are Always Moving Forward or Backward. You Cannot Remain in Place. There Is No Such Thing as Status Quo*

Nothing in the world is static. Everything is in a constant state of change. Even as you read this sentence, cells in your body are dying and being replaced by new ones. You are constantly becoming a new person. Physicists tell us the electrons that form physical mass are constantly whizzing through their orbits at great speed. They never rest.

You don't need a degree in biology to understand that unless a peach is picked and eaten when it's ripe, it begins to rot. We're the same way. If we don't keep moving forward, we'll begin moving backward. In other words, we'll "rot." Time waits for no one. If you're not growing with the passage of time, you're slipping backward.

Focusing on achieving your goals is one of the best ways to keep moving forward. When you set and pursue goals, you are actively creating a new and better life for yourself. If you choose not to set and pursue goals, you are giving up your chance to grow and become. And, if you are not growing, you are dying. There are no in-betweens, and there are no excuses. You either move forward or you move backward. You cannot remain the same as time marches on. The choice is yours. Why not choose growth?

Focus Law #2—*"There Is No Try. There Is Only Do!"*
In the movie, *The Return of the Jedi*, Luke Skywalker crashed his ship in a remote area. His teacher, Yoda, tells him that he can raise it from the mud and muck with the power of his mind. Luke tries and tries and cannot seem to do it. He complains to Yoda who tells him, "There is no try. There is only do." How true.

So many of us spend our entire lives trying without ever really accomplishing anything significant. Saying "I'll try" is noncommittal. It means you don't really believe you can do it. If you did believe you could do it, you'd say, "Sure, I'll get it done." Try simply gives you an excuse for when you don't get it done—you'll just say "I tried." Quit trying and *start doing!*

Ask yourself, "Is what I'm doing right now working for me or against me? Am I growing or disintegrating?" If you're tempted to procrastinate and you know what you need to do to reach your goal, tell yourself... *"DO IT NOW!"*

Focus Law #3—*You Can Achieve Your Goal Only When You Have a Strong Enough Reason to Achieve It. You Need a Big Enough Dream!*

One of the main reasons most people get "out of focus" so easily when they just try to achieve their goals is that they reverse the order of reasons and answers. Reasons need to come first, and answers second.

Until you have a big enough reason for achieving a goal, you will not be motivated to take the action necessary to achieve it. When you have a strong enough reason—a big enough dream—you will focus and take the action almost automatically.

Let's say your goal is to earn enough money to be able to buy a new house with cash. One of your friends asks you why you want to do that. You tell him, "Oh, I just think it would be nice to have a new house and I'm kinda ready for a change of scenery." If that's your reason, do you think you'd be motivated enough to do what it takes to earn the money you need to buy the house? Now, let's say you put this law to work and begin thinking about *WHY* you *really want* the new house.

The next time your friend asks, you could tell him this: "My dream is to have a big new house with a three-car garage, a large master bedroom on the first floor, three bedrooms on the second floor, and a big attractively landscaped yard. My family and I deserve it. We can use the study to help our kids with their homework. And once we're financially free, my wife and I will be able to spend more time with our children playing in the yard, and doing more things together. The kids will also be thrilled to have their friends over to this beautiful home.

"When I move my family into this house, I'll feel good about how well I am providing for them. The children will have a safe, happy place to live that will remove them from the influence of drugs, violence, and alcohol. My wife and I will be able to snuggle up together in front of the fireplace in the winter, and sit on the porch swing, holding hands, in the summer. Our neighbors are upbeat, positive people, like us, and nice to be around. That's *why* I must have this new house."

What if you had motivation like that? Wouldn't you be more likely to go out and advance in your field of endeavor, and do whatever it takes to achieve your goals so you could live your dream? I would certainly hope so.

When your dream is strong enough, you will find a way to achieve it. For example, you may already be in a business or profession that can serve you as the "vehicle" to drive to your dreams. You may just need to reschedule or eliminate some of the activities you're now involved with—so you can focus.

When you begin the goal-setting process, keep this in mind. Focus on your dream and you will find a way to achieve your goals. When you have a strong enough focus, you'll figure out how to do whatever it takes to live your dream.

Focus Law #4—*Fall in Love with Something You Really Want and MUST Have*

To stay focused, it's essential that you decide what you *want* and *MUST have*, not just what you need or think you can have. Your wants are much more powerful motivators than your needs. They serve as a driving force to help you achieve your goals.

Since you almost always get what you expect, you need to raise your level of expectation. Remember this—*your thoughts determine what you put into your subconscious.* It then turns your thoughts into images, which trigger emotions that lead to the actions which cause your results.

Expect more, get more. Expect less, get less. It sounds simple, and it is! Focus on what you want and expect to get it.

That's why poverty is a state of mind, not a state of the pocketbook. Expect to be wealthy and imagine yourself as already wealthy in your mind. It will then be only a matter of time, focus and effort before you become wealthy in your pocketbook.

Someone once said, *"I've never been poor, only broke. Being poor is a frame of mind. Being broke is only a temporary situation."*

When you fall in love with something you *want and MUST have*, you are harnessing the power of the dream. You're putting it on your side in your quest to turn your want into physical reality. By deciding specifically what you *want and MUST have*, you have *chosen* the thoughts that will enter your conscious mind. This will help create an image of you enjoying your *want and MUST have* in your subconscious.

The emotions you feel when you fall in love with this *want and MUST have* are like kindling for your fire. Once lit, they will illuminate all kinds of other resources. Soon you will be a blazing inferno with fire in your belly, exploding to turn your dream into reality.

Focus Law #5—*No More Time and Energy Is Required to Pursue Success Than Accept Mediocrity*

If you're living in the U.S., or in any other country with a strong economy, you live in levels of comfort and luxury your ancestors couldn't even have dreamed of. For example, even the poorest welfare recipients in the U.S. are many times better off than much of the population in Third World countries. Maybe you're living in a country where free enterprise is fairly new. In that case, you are on quite an adventure.

It is your choice whether to actively pursue and claim your share of the prosperity around you or passively settle for whatever mediocrity comes your way. It takes no more time and effort to pursue success than it does to accept misery.

After all, *misery is a full-time job.* I mean, it's tough for someone to be truly miserable without spending (wasting) at least three hours a day whining; six hours watching TV—including, of course, the negative news—and one hour complaining about how bad the world is treating them. And how about their spending two more hours stuffing their faces and doing other non-productive things to take their minds off how miserable they've become. All that adds up to a 77 hour a week job, just to stay fully miserable in mediocrity!

What would happen if they took all that time and energy and *invested* it solely in goal-achieving activities? Let's see—77 hours a week of goal-achieving activities. I'll bet they'd see some positive results and be fired up! And the great thing is, it wouldn't require any more time or effort than it does to be miserable! Prosperity or mediocrity. Which one are you going to choose? The choice is yours.

You already know you can only move forward or backward; you cannot remain in the same place. You are either going for success or accepting misery and mediocrity. Which do you want to commit your life to? Which choice are you *presently* committing your life to?

Focus Law #6—*Eliminate Your "Pink Elephants"*

Focus on where you want to go and what you want to be, not where you don't want to go or what you don't want to be. Get out a pen or highlighter right now and mark this phrase: *Your mind cannot act on the opposite of an idea.*

When you say you don't want something, your mind misses the don't and goes to work to create exactly what you say you don't want. The classic example is a pink elephant. "Don't think of a pink elephant." What did you just think of? A pink elephant, of course. The same concept works in all areas of your life:

> If you say, "I don't want to get sick," what are you focusing on? Sickness.
> If you say, "I want to get out of debt," what are you focusing on? Debt.
> If you say, "I want to get out of paying rent," what are you focusing on? Rent.
> If you say, "I don't want to be fat anymore," what are your focusing on? Obesity.

In all of these cases, what is in control? What you *don't* want and are afraid of getting. And if it's in control, what do you think you're going to get? Everything you don't want!

Start thinking about what you *want* in your life. As you do, you'll begin to "see the light"; you are learning, or reinforcing the key steps to turning your life around; you are ready to break free from the ties that have bound you to the past.

How do you get rid of the last of the ties that bind you? Flip-flop your thinking. Focus on what you *do* want; not what you don't want. Think about where you *want* to go; not where you don't want to go or where you've already been.

Think, "I am healthy... I am wealthy and successful... I have positive, loving relationships... I have a lean, trim body." If you have trouble believing those phrases when you say them, modify them to say, "I am getting healthier every day... I am increasing my wealth and success daily... My relationships are becoming more positive and loving all the time... My body is becoming healthier every day." Either way, the result is the same. You are focusing your mind on what you *do* want in your life.

Your conscious thoughts are putting images into your subconscious mind. And being the dutiful servant it is, it starts going to work to help you turn those images into physical reality. It does not rephrase them or alter them in any way. It just accepts the exact orders it has been given.

Give your subconscious the correct orders through repetition and emotion. *Focus on what you want with your heart and soul.* Create pictures of the life you are moving toward. Trust in the power of your mind to do its part in driving you to turn your dreams into reality.

Doing this sets your mind on your goal like the homing system in a missile. As you move toward your target, "turbulence" may occasionally put you off course, but your focus will come to the rescue. It will always get you smoothly back on track to making a reality of the picture you're focusing on.

Focus Law #7—*Your Barriers Are Imaginary. Ignore Them!*

Believing you have to "break through" barriers is one of the biggest traps you can fall into when you're thinking about making a quantum leap toward your goals. In the past, you may have held yourself back because you *thought* it was going to be too much work to "knock down the walls" you *believed* were preventing you from living your dreams. This whole notion is based on the common, but false, paradigm that these barriers even exist.

In reality, there are no true barriers in your life! *The only "barriers" that stand between you and your goals are those you have put up yourself by faulty thinking and a lack of knowledge.* As General Chuck Yeager, first man to break the so-called "sound barrier," once said: "There should have been a bump on the road, something to let you know you had just punched a nice clean hole through that sonic barrier. (It) was like a poke through Jello. Later on, I realized that this mission had to end in a let-down, because the real barrier wasn't in the sky, but in our knowledge and experience of supersonic flight."

There is always a way to achieve your goals, you just may not be aware of it yet. Therefore, every single barrier you encounter is simply one you built through a false belief in your own mind. And, if you've built a wall, you can surely take it down or walk around it—instantly and permanently. All it takes is a decision. Decide immediately that, from now on, you will live with the belief that, *all my barriers are imaginary, so I am perfectly free to ignore them.*

Say it out loud, "Every barrier I think is between me and my goal is purely a figment of my imagination. Since I created these barriers in my mind, and that is the only place they exist, I am free to un-create them—now and forever. From this moment forward, I choose to ignore my so-called barriers and pursue my dreams relentlessly and with passion in my heart."

Now repeat it three more times, saying it a bit louder each time, until it begins to be ingrained in your mind and you start believing it.

Focus Law #8—*What You Do Is More Important Than How You Do It*

You could be the absolute best in the entire world at what you are now doing. But you would still never achieve your goals, if what you're doing is inconsistent with achieving them.

What if Babe Ruth, the famous baseball player, had dedicated his life to becoming the best in the entire world at mowing the lawn? He would never have won a World Series ring or enjoyed the thrill of hitting a ninth-inning home run. In fact, we probably would never have heard of him.

Keep this in mind as you focus on your dream. *What* you're doing is more important than *how* you're doing it. One of the major reasons most people aren't succeeding nearly as much as they could is because they're spending too much time doing things that simply can't get them where they want to go.

You may habitually be doing what you have learned to do best instead of finding the best things to do. If what you already do best, like your current job, had enabled you to live your dream, you probably wouldn't be reading this book! You may very well be near the top of the "ladder," but is it leaning against the wrong building?

What two or three things, when you do them consistently *every day,* would almost guarantee your success? Shuffling papers, watching TV, reading the newspaper, opening mail, mowing the lawn and other such time-wasters are *not* the things that will make a difference in your success. At best, they are maintenance activities which can often be eliminated or delegated to others. *Be productive, not just busy.*

Did you know that some people think so much about doing something, instead of just doing it, that they wear themselves out!

Remember, *what you do is more important than how you do it.*

I repeat that point because it is so important. You can be rather average, skill and knowledge-wise, but when you do enough of the right things, you'll succeed anyway.

Get out a piece of paper now and write down the two or three things that will make the biggest impact on your success. Commit to doing them every day.

Focus Law #9—*Think in Terms of Making an Investment*

You may get bogged down in the goal-achievement process because you're focusing on what you think you're missing out on when you spend time or money in setting and achieving goals. You may have the attitude that "Gee, it's Saturday morning and I just love sleeping in. Why bother getting up early to exercise, and plan and review my goals, when I could be resting? After all, I worked hard all week and I deserve a break."

How about changing your thinking and focusing on your dream? Consider the time you put into your plans and goals as an *investment* in your future. You were diligent on the job for your employer, now it's time to be diligent for you. Picture yourself investing two hours every day, 14 hours a week, working toward your dream. That's about 8 percent of the total hours in your week. Isn't creating a better future worth investing 8 percent of your time? How serious are you about what you say you want? This is a good place to start.

Here's another area where people make a mistake. They think the money they spend on positive books and tapes, seminars, and other continuing education activities are costs. They're not! And while these things are certainly optional, that doesn't mean they're not essential for your success! After all, success *is* optional!

A cost is money you spend for a one-time return. An investment, on the other hand, is money you put to work to generate returns for many years to come. Continuing education and training are some of the best investments you will ever make in yourself. Why?

Let's say you *invest* $500 to attend a seminar. You get one good idea from it and get fired up enough to use that idea to earn an extra $50 a week. In five years, you will have earned $13,000 extra income on your $500 investment. That's a return of 2,600 percent! Compare that to the $138 you would have earned on a government issued bond or certificate of deposit that compounded at 5 percent annually. Your $500 grew to only $638 in five years. That's a return of only 27 percent! Which is the better investment?

Even if you had to attend five $500 seminars to get that one good idea, you would still generate many times more income than putting the money in the bank or buying a government bond. And, who can put a price tag on developing an increased awareness of what it takes to be successful? More enthusiasm, greater peace of mind and hope, more loving relationships with your family, and more happiness, are all benefits. Even if you gained only *one* of these benefits, wouldn't it be worth it?

What better investment could you make than in yourself and your family? Think of the time and money you put into continuing education and setting and achieving goals as the best investments you will ever make. This will help keep you on the right track, and focused on achieving your goals.

Focus Law #10—*Your Mind Works According to "Rules." Obey the Rules if You Want to Succeed!*

Have you ever set a goal, put together a plan that would enable you to achieve it, started to execute it, and then wondered why it seemed like you weren't getting anywhere? What probably happened was, somewhere along the line, you didn't follow the rules. Your mind works according to rules and ignoring them never produces desirable results.

Here Are The Five "Rules of the Mind"

1. Your mind doesn't care about time. It doesn't understand future tense. And when your mind doesn't understand something, it can't go to work to create it.

Always write and think about your goals in the present tense. Saying you'll accomplish something in the future is procrastination. And someday becomes a new word called never! Think, "I am now earning $100,000 a year," instead of "I will be earning $100,000 a year in five years." The "now" statement puts your mind to work *now* to turn your goals into reality. It keeps you from limiting your mind by putting artificial time limits on your goals. After all, you may be able to earn $100,000 a year in two years, when you let your mind go to work to figure out how. It also helps you enjoy the process of pursuing your goals as much as the momentary feelings of triumph of achieving them.

2. Your mind can't go to work to help you create the *opposite* of something i.e., a negatively-phrased statement. Tell it, "I want to get out of debt," and it will actually focus on helping you stay in debt. It glosses right over the not part of your statement and focuses on debt! Instead think, "I pay cash for everything and I'm financially free." You always need to state what you want in positive terms, not what you don't want.

3. Your mind doesn't accept ultimatums, demands or the use of force. Have you ever told yourself, "I'll get thin or I won't go to the party next weekend," or "I'll get out of debt, even if it kills me?" While statements like that certainly place the power of emotion on your side, they don't work, because your mind is impartial. It doesn't accept ultimatums.

Saying "I will" do something violates the first rule—your mind can't react to future tense. And statements like "even if it kills me" are unwise. How come? Well, what do you think your mind begins focusing on?

4. Your subconscious accepts anything put into it as real. This is why your thoughts are so extremely important. You can run around all day saying out loud you are successful and it will help you achieve your goal. But if you keep telling yourself you're worthless and you'll never live your dream, that's the image that forms in your subconscious. It will then act as the dutiful servant it is, accept your statement at face value, and go to work to turn it into physical reality.

Fortunately, the opposite is true, as well. Since your subconscious accepts anything you put into it as real, you can picture your successes by thinking about them in the present tense. This is why present tense thinking is so effective. Every time you feel successful or think successful thoughts, you are creating success blueprints in your mind.

When you go to achieve a new, lofty goal, your mind sorts through all the images it has. It then discovers you already have success blueprints indicating you can achieve that goal. Your goal-achievement then matches the image that is already in your mind and the process becomes easier and habitual.

5. Your mind gives you exactly what you dwell on. Just as it accepts anything put into it as real, your mind will drive you to create, in physical reality, exactly what you dwell upon in your intellectual and emotional states. And remember this:

- ◆ Focus on success and you'll get success.
- ◆ Focus on failure and you'll get failure.
- ◆ Focus on nothing and you'll get nothing.

Be crystal-clear about exactly what it is you want because, whatever it is, that's most likely what you're going to get!

Focus Law #11—*Success Compounds Over Time*

Success is similar to a stock investment; it can compound over time. Unlike a stock, however, you can determine at what rate and how frequently your success compounds. When you make small, steady gains in any area of your life, they can compound into huge returns in a relatively short time.

For example, when you become just one percent better at doing something every day, over the course of a year, you could improve your effectiveness by almost 38 times! Imagine that. For instance, you could start improving your ability to lead others by one percent a day. When you consistently make those small gains, you would be nearly 38 times more effective as a leader one year from today! What could that do for your success?

Have you ever wanted to really make it big in your career or business? Have you ever thought you would never be good enough at it to be a leader? Change your thinking. Improving yourself by just one percent every day could make you 38 times better or more effective in one year.

Have you ever seriously wanted to significantly increase your income? Figure out what you can do today to increase your income by just one percent. For example, if your average earnings are now $100 a day, figure out what you would need to do to make an extra dollar today. If you could keep increasing your income by one percent each day, you'd be earning $3,778 per day by the end of one year!

That's how fortunes are made. When you consistently take one "baby step" after another, every day, they begin to add up. Your momentum toward success increases and you eventually realize your dream. What often looks like "an over night success" is simply an accumulation of many small steps over time.

Always believe your dream is possible, no matter how big it may be.

Here's how Pat Riley coached his team to win their NBA (National Basketball Association in the U.S.) championship. Before the season began, he asked each player to improve by one percent in five key areas. When all 15 players improved by just one percent in those five areas, the team would then be more than twice as good as it was the year before! This is how losing teams can turn into winning teams in a short period of time. It's also how you can turn any group you are associated with into a "championship" team relatively quickly.

Be consistent, persistent and patient, and compound your success. The results could truly amaze you. As Einstein once said, *"Compound interest is man's greatest invention."*

Focus Law #12—*Five Field Goals Beats Two Touchdowns Every Time*

One of the best ways to be sure you reach your goals is to use the concept of *targeting*: always aim for your target or goal and score points every time you get close. This gives you a sense of accomplishment, which allows you to celebrate your growth and enjoy the process. To illustrate this idea, here's an interesting example from the world of sports:

The Dallas Cowboys football team are playing the Green Bay Packers. Each time the Cowboys get the ball, their goal is to score a touchdown. However, they're having some trouble cracking the Green Bay defense. And, in fact, they don't score a single touchdown the entire game. Even so, they do end up kicking five field goals.

Green Bay, of course, has the same goal—score a touchdown every time they have the football. They are more successful than Dallas because they put the ball in the endzone twice during the game. Unfortunately for them, the Cowboys' consistency in scoring little victories—field goals—five times, paid off. Dallas won the game 15-14!

Achieving your goals works the same way. Consistent small victories will lead to your ultimate victory. Remember, five field goals beats two touchdowns every time.

Focus Law #13—*Do the Important Things First and the So-Called "Urgent" Things Later*

Have you ever felt as though some sort of emergency always came up just when you were ready to get started on your goals? Most people create emergencies on a regular basis and use them as convenient excuses to never pursue their dreams. Here's how to make sure you don't join them:

Live your life *on purpose*. Think of all your actions in terms of your mission and values. *Do the important things first and the so-called "urgent" things later.*

Here's that sentence again, because it's a key to your success. Do the important things first and the so-called urgent things later. The important things are those that lead you closer to your goals and dreams and are in harmony with your mission and values. Focus on them and you will find that most of the so-called urgent things seem to get done by themselves.

To keep the difference between urgent and important straight in your mind, ask yourself, "Will doing this seemingly urgent task really matter much in five years? Or is doing something to move me closer to my dreams and goals more important?"

When you're living *on purpose*, it will mean far more to you to be doing things toward living your dream than to mow the lawn or pull the weeds. Doing whatever it takes to be living your dream helps you expand and grow into a richer, fuller, happier, and more complete person. It's highly unlikely you could say the same thing about yard work!

Say mowing the lawn or pulling the weeds still seems important to you and you have no one else in your family to delegate these jobs to. Set a new goal for yourself: earn enough extra income so you can pay someone else to do those chores for you. Whatever you pay someone to do them will be worth it. You'll be freeing up more of your precious time and mental energy so you can invest it in pursuing your goals and living your dream.

You will never *find* time to set and achieve your goals; you must *make* time for them. It's a deliberate, conscious choice. Do the important things first. Leave the urgent things for later, or delegate them to a family member, or pay someone else to do them. You'll then find it's much easier to make time for achieving your goals.

Focus Law #14—*Do the Right Things and Go for Results*

If you keep doing the same old things while expecting different results, you'll be disappointed. It doesn't much matter how long it takes you to achieve your goal, as long as you're consistently doing your best toward achieving it. If you don't reach a goal in the time you originally set, simply reset it. What matters most is that you keep going for the result. In the process you will grow and become the person you need to be in order to accomplish the goal.

Say your goal is to reach a particular level in your business or profession in a certain number of months. You need to do specific things to accomplish that. For example, you may need to meet some new prospects and cultivate more relationships.

Also, you'll probably want to counsel with your leader or mentor so he can help you develop a specific game plan. After that, you may want to meet with him periodically to help you stay on track and resolve any challenges you may need help on.

As Parkinson's Law states, "The amount of work will always expand to fill the time allotted to it." By managing results and not time, the extra momentum you build up as you get "cranking," will enable you to grow yourself faster and live your dream sooner. Keep doing as much as you can and don't worry about the time.

To stay focused—manage results, not time. Time just is and it keeps marching on. Set goals that can be broken down into measurable results. *Commit to the results you want, not to spending a certain amount of time working toward them.*

This is the biggest difference between true successes and everyone else. Achievers commit to *results*, while others only commit to being busy. Results count; busyness doesn't. *Commit to results. Be productive, not just busy.*

Focus Law #15—*You Are Already Ready to Start, So Just Do It—NOW!*

You can spend your entire life getting ready to be ready, and you'll never be ready. All of the potential you will ever have is already inside of you. The only way you will ever know what you're truly capable of is by doing things you've never done before. How do you do that? By doing something that moves you toward your dream. Take the first step and keep going. That's all it takes to get moving and growing.

Put one foot in front of the other. Put your right foot out. Put your left foot out. Put your right foot out. Put your left foot out. Soon you'll be walking around the room. Put your right foot out faster. Put your left foot out faster. Put your right foot out faster. Put your left foot out faster. Soon you'll be running down the hall. Put your right foot out even faster. Put your left foot out even faster. Put your right foot out even faster. Put your left foot out even faster. Soon you'll be winning every race you run. But you'll never win any race unless you begin it.

Step up to the starting gate. You are ready to win. So just do it—*now!*

Chapter 10

Build A Picture Of Your Dream

"Whether we spend life winning or losing depends on how we use our mindsight—what we choose to 'see' or to 'dream.'"
Dr. David J. Schwartz

Determine Your Direction

One of the biggest reasons people have trouble staying focused is they don't really know exactly what they want. They constantly change their minds and go off pursuing a new goal—before they've ever achieved their previous one. This flitting from one goal to another goes on for years until they become so frustrated they quit setting goals altogether.

The way to get around this situation is to first invest a little time determining exactly what you want and which direction you want to move in. You'll have a much easier time staying focused on going in that direction and achieving your goals.

Quick! What Do You Really Want Out of Life?

If you're like most people, you may have trouble answering that question, especially when put on the spot like that. Many would say something like "To have a family."

Well, with an indefinite goal like that, you could achieve it by getting "a family" of rodents to reside in your house.

"But that's not what I meant," you say.

Well, that's what you said.

Your subconscious mind is quite literal. It takes what you tell it at face value. In order to stay focused on meaningful goals, you need to know *exactly* what you want and *why* you want it. You then need to communicate this information accurately and repeatedly to your subconscious so it can help you get it.

Here's a procedure to figure out exactly what you want and what goals you need to set:

Defining Your Dream

To define your dream, you need to answer these basic questions:

- Where are you now? Where are you starting from?
- Where do you want to be? What's your dream?
- Why do you want to be there? Why do you want to live your dream?

In order to answer these questions thoroughly, we are going to re-visit some of the thought processes that you used earlier in the book to create your *Dreambuilding Book.*

Dream Defining Step 1—*Where Are You Now? Where Are You Starting From?*

As we discussed before, in order to develop a sound plan for going forward to where you want to be, you need to know where you're starting from. In Chapter 1, you had an opportunity to give yourself a quick rating and answer some questions about some key areas of your life. Now give yourself a "Personal Success Check-Up" in these areas, by answering the following questions in writing. Take your time and really put some serious thought into this process.

- How is your family life? How would you like it to be? Are you able to spend as much time as you'd like to with your family?

♦ How is your business or profession coming along? Are you growing as a person? What is your level of commitment? *Are you doing something every day, firmly focused on your dream?* Are you excited about your future? Do you "have your hands on" a vehicle you can drive all the way to your dream? Are you consistently meeting new people and building relationships? What can you do to build your future that you're not now doing?

♦ How's your income? Do you have residual income—the kind you receive whether you do anything or not? Are you living up to your potential, income-wise? If not, why? What income level do you want? What are you doing to make that happen? Would you like to be able to provide more for your family?

♦ What's your financial situation? What do you own free and clear of debt? Do you have any debt? If so, how much? If some of it's credit card debt, have you shopped around to get the best interest rate? Have you developed a plan to eliminate your debt? What's your plan for retirement? Are you "all set" to live comfortably, or do you plan to just keep on working as long as you can? Do you realize residual income is like having a large sum of money in the bank generating interest? How would that feel—to have a steady stream of residual income?

♦ What's your time situation? Are you focusing on maximizing each day's activities—so that, step-by-step, you're always moving closer to your dream? Are you living "on-purpose," and in line with your mission? Would you like to free-up more time to do what you enjoy the most? Are you investing your time in working toward your dream? If not, how come? What can you do to eliminate time "wasters"? Do you watch TV? How much? Do you need to redirect your energies to build your future? What chores can you delegate? Are you doing things other family members can do or that you could hire out—like mowing the lawn?

After answering those questions, do you have a better idea of how you'd answer the question, "Where am I now?"

When you're done, go back and compare your answers to the ones you wrote down in Chapter 1, where you rated your life in these various areas. Has anything changed?

Dream Defining Step 2—*Where Do You Want to Go? What's Your Dream?*

For most people, that's a tough question. Most can usually tell you exactly where they *don't* want to go. But it's often difficult for them to describe exactly where they *do* want to go. They think of all the things they don't want—instead of focusing on their dreams and goals and exactly what they *do* want.

The result is that it's virtually impossible for them to put together some sort of action plan to make their lives better. It's like the story in *Alice in Wonderland* where Alice comes to the junction in the road that leads in different directions. She doesn't know where she really wants to go, so she asks the Cheshire Cat for advice:

> "Cheshire Cat...would you tell me please, which way I ought to go from here?"
> "That depends a good deal on where you want to get to," the Cat said.
> "I don't much care where...," Alice said.
> "Then it doesn't matter which way you go," the Cat said.

Don't be like Alice. Begin right now to decide exactly where you want to go. Start focusing on your dream.

Dreambuilding

To begin deciding where you want to go, start building your dream. Let go of the past and focus on a future where you are what you want to be and you're living your dream. Build your dream by driving your dream car and looking at your dream home. Put yourself in your new life's picture, surrounded by your family and friends. Dream like a child who believes he can be whatever he wants to be.

Focus on your dream as you'd like it to be. Start believing it's possible for you. No one has any more potential than you do to live your dream. As Thoreau once said, *"If one advances confidently in the direction of his dreams, and endeavors to live the life which he has imagined, he will meet with a success unexpected in common hours."*

Your Dream Life's Questions

Most of us are not used to dreambuilding. We have been "beaten up" for years and told we can't do this, or there's no way we'll ever have that. You already know those are lies. You *can* do whatever you decide you want to do, have whatever you want to have, and be whatever you want to be.

Continue the process we started earlier, when you began producing your *Dreambuilding Book*, by answering these questions, in writing:

- ♦ What would I do if I knew I couldn't fail? Success is a given and failure is impossible.
- ♦ If I could accomplish any three things, what would they be?
- ♦ If I could be as successful as I wanted to be, what level or position would I reach?
- ♦ If I could travel anywhere I wanted, where would I go?
- ♦ If I could live anywhere in the world, where would it be?

- If I could live in any house I wanted, what would it look like?
- If I could drive any vehicle I wanted, what would I drive?
- If I could dress any way I wanted, what would I wear?
- If I could have any five material things, what would they be?
- If I could have the perfect family life, what would it be like?
- If I had all the time I wanted, to do what I want to do, what would I be doing?
- If I could meet anyone I wanted, who would I meet and where would we be?
- If I could earn as much money as I wanted, how much would I earn?
- If I could experience anything I wanted, what things would I experience?
- If I could learn anything I wanted, what would I learn?
- If I could found or contribute to three causes, what would they be?
- If I could solve any problem in my life and in the world, what would they be?
- If someone gave me $10 million today, what would I do with it?
- If I could have any three wishes, what would I wish for? (You may not wish for more wishes!)
- What are the three most unusual things I would like to do or have? (Don't worry about what others may think about you. They're probably not thinking about you anyway. But even if they are, it doesn't matter.)

Now get out a few more clean sheets of paper and think about your answers to those questions as you describe living your dream.

♦ What would my perfect day, week, or month be like? Where would I be? Who would I be with? What would I be doing?

♦ In 5 years, what would I like to be doing? What kind of person would I like to have become? Where will I be living? Who will I be spending time with? How much will I be earning? What knowledge will I have acquired? What kinds of experiences will I have had? What will my typical day be like?

♦ In 10 years, what would I like to be doing? What kind of person would I like to have become? Where will I be living? Who will I be spending time with? How much will I be earning? What knowledge will I have acquired? What kinds of experiences will I have had? What will my typical day be like?

♦ In 20 years, what would I like to be doing? What kind of person would I like to have become? Where will I be living? Who will I be spending time with? How much will I be earning? What knowledge will I have acquired? What kinds of experiences will I have had? What will my typical day be like?

♦ In living my dream, what would be my highest desires or goals in each area of life? What 3-5 things would I like to accomplish, more than any other, in each of the following areas: Financial • Business • Personal development • Social, including hobbies • Spiritual • Relationships • Health and fitness, including sports • Material things like houses, cars, boats, planes, and clothes.

♦ Now look at the list you've just created and ask, "What else is *possible*?" Add any totally wild things you've always thought would be great to do. Have you ever wanted to score a touchdown in the Super Bowl or race in the Indianapolis 500 or skate in the Olympics? If so, add them to your list.

♦ Next add your biggest dreams that, at this point, you may not think are possible. Have you ever wanted to make $1,000,000 in a year? Be elected President? Walk on the moon? Put anything on it that would be exciting and rewarding to do.

Reach for Your Dream

You've been focused and working hard and smart. Now you're ready to reach for your dream. Think of your dream as the meal you are selecting from the Menu of Your Life. Since this is a mighty fine restaurant you are dining at this evening, the appetizer, salad, vegetables, bread, beverage, and dessert all come with your meal. Just tell your waitperson which appetizer you want, what dressing you want on your salad, what you would like to drink, and what you want for dessert. They will then put the order in to the chef. Rest assured that when your meal arrives, it will include everything you want.

Think of your dream the same way. It's your main course. When you select it, you will automatically get your appetizer, salad, vegetables, bread, beverage, and dessert. As you achieve your dream, you will automatically achieve many of your other goals in the process.

Staying focused on your dream allows you to gather all the resources available to you to achieve it. Use your resources and focus intently on turning your dream into physical reality in the shortest amount of time possible.

Think of a cowboy out on the range. If his herd is running in every direction, he will wear himself out attempting to get them where he wants them to go—if he tries to round them up alone. However, when he uses all his men and their horses, he benefits from the power of everyone pulling together to effect the roundup of his cattle. When a group of people is focused on the same goal, it'll get done a whole lot quicker.

Another way to think of the benefits of focusing on your dream is to visualize a light. A 100-watt lightbulb in your kitchen radiates a nice soft glow. These same light particles, however, can be gathered and focused so they are all going in the same direction. When this happens, you get a laser beam that can cut diamonds. The same particles of light, when focused, concentrate all the available energy into one thin powerful razor sharp beam.

Focusing on your dream with laser-beam intensity will help you cut through all the inessential stuff. It'll point you to exactly where you want to go. Along the way, you will learn that you can accomplish more than you ever thought possible. In fact, you'll grow and become the person you need to be to live your dream.

For example, let's say you want to build your dream house, take a trip around the world, write a bestselling novel, and spend more time with your family. What dream would be best to choose? That's an individual decision you need to make for yourself. There is no right or wrong dream and no right or wrong goals. You need to choose something that really gets *you* excited.

In this case, one way to *laser-beam focus* your resources would be to choose the affirmation "I am earning $1,000,000 or more this year while living a healthy, balanced life." And do you realize that it's no harder to say $1,000,000 than it is to say $100,000? So why not *dream big*?

When you achieve this big dream, you will naturally be able to build your house, travel around the world, and do whatever else it is you want to do. This will give you the time to concentrate on what's really important to you—*like spending more time with your spouse and family.* As you strive to achieve your overall dream, you'll naturally achieve many of your smaller dreams and goals along the way. That's just the way it works.

Which Dream Will You Reach for?

Get out a piece of paper and think about your dream. Look back over the list of dreams you just completed. Spend a few minutes thinking about them, then organize them as follows:

- ♦ Prioritize your list of dreams. Divide your list into A, B, and C dreams, according to their level of importance to you. A dreams are those you feel you absolutely *want and MUST accomplish* to have reached your goals and live a happy, satisfying, fulfilling life. Include five-to-ten dreams on your A list.
- ♦ Next, develop a B list of dreams you would *love* to accomplish.
- ♦ Finally, put together a C list of dreams that it would be *nice* to accomplish but that you don't get all that fired up about at this point.

Now revise your A list based on your answers to the following questions:

- ♦ Which five dreams would mean the most to you to accomplish?
- ♦ Which five dreams on your list could you get the most emotionally involved in? Which ones "light your fire," either because you believe in them passionately or you would be really fired up to achieve them.
- ♦ In the next five years, pursuing your heart's desire in which area of life—financial, business, relationships, emotional, spiritual, health, or another—would give you the most satisfaction and contribute the most to your overall mission in life?
- ♦ What would you trade your life for? Not what would you die for—but what is important enough that you would trade your waking hours to accomplish it and then feel like the trade was worth it.

Add your answers to these questions to your A list and take off any dreams that are less important to you and place them on your B list. Now, get ready to reach for your *dream*. Before you do, though, read the following section about goals *not* to choose!

Goals You Need to Avoid

You now have a list of possible goals. The next thing we will look at is what things to eliminate from your list, or what goals you should never choose. Here are the guidelines to follow:

◆ **Never Set a Goal to Eliminate Something You Now Have. You'll Just Get More of the Same!**

How many times have you tried to "get rid of a bad habit," "quit smoking," "lose extra weight," or "get out of debt"? How many times have you succeeded at doing it? Probably never. Why?

By setting a goal to eliminate what you already have, you're focusing your thoughts on the very thing you want to get rid of! Remember, your mind can't focus on the opposite of an idea. All it hears is "bad habit," "smoking," "extra weight," or "debt." It then goes to work to *maintain* the very thing you'd like to eliminate!

To illustrate this, imagine you are out in the wilderness, preparing to take a canoe trip on a beautiful river. Being awed by the breathtaking surroundings, you decide you want to enjoy as much of the scenery along the banks as possible.

You have two choices. You can paddle either upstream or downstream. If you go upstream and paddle against the current, you'll either stay in the same place or drift backward. If you go downstream, you'll be using nature's power to help you achieve your goal of seeing as much as possible along the way. You'll also have more energy to paddle around any obstacles, like rocks, and cover even more territory.

Setting goals to achieve your dream works the same way. If you set a goal to eliminate what you already have and focus on it, it would be like paddling upstream. At best, you don't get anywhere! You are ignoring the fact that you imagined the opposite of an idea. Follow the rules of nature, and the mind will help you. Focus on what you want, not what you don't want. Don't spend (waste) any time dwelling on where you are. Be drawn by your dream and go toward the positive.

Another one of nature's laws is that it automatically tries to fill any vacuums. When you eliminate one thing, the "space" doesn't just sit there empty. Nature wants to fill it with something else. One thing is always replaced with another. If you eliminate a bad habit, it is replaced with something else. If you don't replace it with a good habit, it will simply be replaced with another bad habit.

If you eliminate one kind of debt, it will be replaced with another kind of debt—unless you replace the "space" with wise use of money.

If you quit smoking, you will have the urge to begin again—until you replace the old habit with a new, healthier one, such as exercising or reading.

If you lose weight, you'll gain it back—until you replace your old habits with new habits that keep you in shape.

♦ Happiness and Peace of Mind Are Not Goals

Many people make the mistake of setting goals "to be happy" or "to have peace of mind." Happiness and peace of mind are not goals. They are conditions of life. They come as a result of the personal growth and the person you become by doing the things necessary to reach your goals.

For example, let's say your goal is to become a millionaire in five years. Since money is a reward for services rendered or products sold, there's only one way you can do this without violating nature's laws—provide enough service or products so that others will reward you with enough money in the next five years for you to have $1,000,000 by then.

How could you provide this service or these products? If you're in sales, sell more products to your existing customers. If you're an engineer, design more products and improve the existing ones. You are then rewarded based on the number of people you help who use the products and services available through your efforts.

Would you agree that when you are focusing on helping others, you'll be growing as a person? Would you also agree that as you grow and help other people, you'll more likely be happy and enjoy peace of mind as a result? This is the natural order of this cause and effect relationship. Stretching for your goals causes you to grow, which causes you to live with a higher level of awareness. The effect of this whole process is increased happiness, peace of mind and more success, as you live your dream.

Choose Your Dream

Now, you are ready to choose your dream. Here are some questions for you to answer:

- What single dream are you most passionate about achieving?
- Look at your A list of dreams. What one *dream* will help you achieve the largest number or most important of your A list dreams? For example, it may be becoming financially free and building your dream home.
- Write your *Dream* here:

- Write "My Dream" across the top of a sheet of paper. Below it, write out your Dream in big, bold letters.

That's your "main course". Now you're going to learn how to decide if this is really what you want to order. Then you'll learn how to order your main course so that you can be assured of getting exactly what you want.

Dream Defining Step 3—*WHY Do You Want to Be There? WHY Do You Want to Live Your Dream?*

As you've already learned, in order to achieve your goals in the most efficient manner possible, you need to become emotionally involved with them. Reasons come first, answers second. *When the "why" gets strong enough, you'll figure out the "how."*

Now picture yourself living your dream:

- ◆ Can you clearly see yourself on the movie screen of your mind, living your dream?
- ◆ Do you seriously want to achieve your dream?
- ◆ Is this the most desirable, most exciting dream you can think of to achieve?

If you answered no to any of those questions, you need to re-think your dream. You probably have done one of these three things:

- ◆ You may have chosen a dream you think you "should" choose, because of what society, your family or friends said you can or cannot do. This will lead to problems sooner or later. Instead, you need to choose the dream *you* really, really want to go for, because of what you feel and believe deep down inside you. Remember, no one can live your life for you, and you know what's in your heart better than anyone else.
- ◆ You may have chosen a dream that is too small. It doesn't really get you fired up enough to do whatever it

takes for you to grow and overcome the obstacles you'll encounter in order to achieve it.

♦ You may have chosen a dream that is too big for your present belief level. If you absolutely cannot see yourself achieving your goal, lower it slightly until you can see yourself achieving it. If you can't imagine living in a $1,000,000 house, lower it to one that would cost $500,000 or $250,000. And remember, whatever you *truly* believe is what's realistic for you.

Be careful about lowering your dream too far, though. Remember, this is *your* dream. Once you have chosen it you'll be 100 percent focused on it and, in all likelihood, will *not* be changing it. You have incredible reservoirs of talent inside you that have never been tapped. Successful people will tell you that you really can't dream too big. And remember that anything you can imagine and truly believe in is possible for you to achieve.

Since you have already conceived your dream, you need to believe it to be what you really truly want. So start raising your belief level to where you can focus and start working toward achieving your dream.

"How" Just Doesn't Matter

You may not realize all the resources available to you or how they could be combined to help you achieve your dream. And it just doesn't matter.

It's unreasonable to think you should now know exactly *how* you're going to make your dream come true. You may have a general idea of how, such as by building your business or career. You may also know the next step you will take. That's great. However, you cannot predict every single thing that needs to occur before you achieve your dream.

If you think you already know exactly how to achieve your dream, go back to the prior section and choose a bigger dream; it's just not big enough! *The whole purpose of your dreams and goals is to cause you to stretch, grow and become the best person you can be.* If you already know all the things you need to do to achieve your dream, you are not stretching and growing. You need a bigger dream.

You may say, "I know I need to grow myself personally and build my business or profession to achieve my dream." However, you don't know how many people you'll need to meet, how many books you'll need to read, how many tapes you'll need to listen to, how many courses you'll need to take, or how many seminars you'll need to attend. So yes, you basically know what you need to do overall.

But your "success equation," which is "whatever it takes to get the job done," has yet to be unveiled. And, the bottom line is, it just doesn't matter. You'll figure it out along the way.

The *True Test* for Your Dream

You have conceived your dream and clearly defined it. You can picture yourself living it. You believe you can have it, although you don't know exactly what it'll take to get it. And now it's time to give your dream the *True Test* to determine whether this is the right dream for you. This test consists of three parts:

1. Your Reason *Why*.
2. The Growth Factor.
3. The Value Match

Your Reason Why—*The First Part of the True Test*

Go back to the paper where you wrote the description of your dream. Below it write, "Why I want and deserve to live my dream." Then write, in as much detail as you can, *exactly why* you want and deserve to live your dream:

- What pleasure will you get from achieving it?
- What pain will you experience if you don't achieve it?
- What other goals will achieving this dream naturally cause you to accomplish?
- What else will achieving this dream allow you to be, do, and have?

What makes you the happiest and most excited about living this dream? If you don't have a good reason *why* you want to live your dream, it has failed the *True Test*.

Purpose is stronger than object. You can certainly set a goal to build a $1,000,000 house. However, you'll never take the actions necessary to earn the income to enable you to build it until you have a strong enough reason *why* you want to live in it. If you don't have a big enough reason why, you won't be motivated enough by your dream.

The Growth Factor—*The Second Part of the True Test*

Now that you have defined the reasons why you want to live your dream, write down your answer to this question:

- What kind of person do I need to become in order to live my dream?

Once you've described the kind of person you need to become, you can complete this section of the *True Test* by answering these questions:

- Is this the kind of person I would like to become?
- Is this the kind of person in harmony with my values and my mission?

If you answered yes to both questions, your dream has passed the second part of the *True Test*.

The Value Match—*The Final Part of the True Test*

Many people never live their dreams because they allow themselves to lose sight of what really matters. They may realize this, but tell themselves they just can't help it. They may achieve their goals but will suffer from a profound sense of emptiness inside because the goals they have achieved conflict with their values.

This sense of emptiness is their heart's way of telling them that something is not congruent in their life. They do not have laser-beam focus on their dream, because they are moving toward goals that do not match their values.

When you put your exterior affairs in the proper perspective, by aligning them with your values, you will enjoy your success as well as achieve it. To live your dream and have a wonderful life, be sure the goals you set are congruent with your values—*before* you begin your quest.

To be sure your dream passes the Value Match, ask yourself these four questions:

1. Is the reason you want material things valid? If you wrote down that you wanted a new house to make you happy, you're off track. You'll never be happy. Material things are not the source of your happiness. The house could give you an outlet for creative expression or be a warm, cozy place to share love with your family, but it, in and of itself, will not cause you to be happy. Neither will any other material possession.

2. Does your dream and your reasons for achieving it match your values?

3. When you achieve your dream will you be able to live in line with your values?

4. Are your activities in line with your dream? For instance, partying every night and becoming an Olympic gold medallist are not compatible. When you find activities that are out of line, it probably means

you're not clear about what your values really are. Go back to the section on determining your values, beliefs, and life purpose and study it again.

If you answered yes to all four questions, your dream passed the *True Test*. Congratulations!

Chapter 11

Turn Your Dream Into An Achievable Goal

"Choosing a goal and sticking to it changes everything."
Scott Reed

The 4-Step Process for Achieving Your Goals

In the last section, you chose a dream. And, now that you have a "vehicle" to achieve it, you need to do whatever it takes. You may not know exactly what it'll take, but it just doesn't matter. As Paul "Bear" Bryant, legendary Alabama football coach once said, *"My attitude has always been...if it's worth playing, it's worth paying the price to win."* The dream you chose is just that—a dream. Now it's time to turn your dream into a true goal—*a Dream Goal.*

Get out a new sheet of paper and rewrite your dream by keeping these points in mind:

Goal-Achievement Step #1—*Write Your Dream in the Present Tense*

Phrase it as: "I have..." "I now..." or "I am..." and then your goal. Some examples: "I have earned $1,000,000;" "I have built my dream house on the water;" "I am spending two hours a day with my family;" "I now make $100,000 per year." Using the present tense "tricks" your subconscious into believing it and helps you achieve your goal more quickly.

When your subconscious gets the message that you have already done something, it goes searching through its files to figure out when you did it. Of course, it comes up "empty-handed" since you haven't done it yet. Being the ever-obedient servant that it is, it then decides, "Oh, gee, if he thinks he's already done this thing and I can't find any record of having achieved it, I must have missed one of my orders somewhere along the line. I'd better go to work immediately and create that record so I don't get into trouble for not obeying orders." Your subconscious then puts the "gears" in motion that will help you turn your dream into reality.

If you make the common mistake of phrasing your goal in the future tense, as for example, "I will make $1,000,000", it does not serve as a catalyst to get the gears spinning. Your subconscious thinks, "Oh, maybe he'll make $1,000,000…someday. I know he hasn't done it yet, but maybe he'll do it sometime in the future. I'll just sit back and take it easy until he does."

The result is, of course, that it just doesn't happen. "Someday" turns into a new word called "never," and your dream fades into oblivion.

Goal-Achievement Step #2—*Give Your Dream an Exact Date for Its Achievement*

To transform your dream into an effective goal, you *must* have a date for its achievement. How do you choose the date? As you've probably heard before, most people overestimate what they can do in a decade and underestimate what they can do in a year.

The goal-achievement process works like a farmer planting a crop. When he picked his Dream Goal, he chose the seed to plant. Once he's planted it, he waters the crop and tends to it until it is ready to harvest.

The major difference between achieving your Dream Goal and harvesting a crop is that the farmer knows almost exactly *when* the crop will be ready to harvest. Each seed has a gestation period—the time from planting to harvest. Your Dream Goal also has a gestation period but, unfortunately, you don't know how long it will take for you to achieve it. What's the answer? Take your best guess at the approximate gestation period for harvesting your goal. After all, you've probably never pursued your Dream Goal before. How could you possibly know how long it will take?

Choose the date when you *want* to achieve your goal, even if you're not sure whether you *can* achieve it *by* that time. Choosing when *you want to* achieve your goal keeps you from giving yourself too much time to harvest your crop. If you have too much time, it will lessen your incentive to work on your "farm." If that were so, there's a good chance your "crops" will rot before you harvest your fields.

It's like the farmer who sits around thinking, "Oh, yes, those crops will take five years to grow so there's no need to water them today. I can always do it tomorrow." What the farmer failed to realize is that his time frame for the crop was way off. He thinks his crop will take five years to mature. Actually, his crops, if properly cared for, would be ready to harvest that fall. Since he keeps putting off the action he needs to take, his crops will end up rotting in the field and he will never realize the joy of a healthy harvest.

Goal-Achievement Step #3—*Give Your Dream Goal Some "BAMS"!*

The next key to transforming your dream into a workable goal is to give it some *"BAMS."* It needs to be *Believable, Achievable, Measurable,* and *Specific.*

Believable—You need to have a *believable* goal. You need to believe it's possible to achieve your Dream Goal. Notice I said, *you* need to believe it. It doesn't matter what anyone else thinks. If you don't sincerely believe that it's at least *possible* to achieve your Dream Goal, you will never consistently take the actions and develop the skills necessary to turn it into reality.

Achievable—Your goal needs to be *achievable*. If you choose a Dream Goal that can never be attained, it would be impossible to stay motivated to work toward it. And, if you won't keep working toward it until you achieve it, there's no reason to even bother setting it in the first place. That is why perfection isn't a workable goal. You could work all your waking hours for the rest of your life and you would never achieve perfection! Instead, strive for maximum excellence—not perfection.

Never phrase your goal like "I have become the best possible dancer in the world." No matter how good you are, you can always get better! Therefore, you will never achieve your goal. Besides, how would you ever know if you were the best dancer? Who decides that? You, your audience, or the press? What criteria do they use? How can you rank every dancer in the world? You don't even know how to list all the dancers in the world, much less figure out which ones are better or worse than you.

Comparing yourself to others is a trap—some are doing better than you and some are doing worse. Instead, *only compare yourself now with the way you want to be.*

Measurable—Make sure your goal is *measurable*. If you cannot measure your Dream Goal, you will never know if you've achieved it. "I have become financially free," is not measurable. Does financially free mean a $1,000,000 net worth, a $100,000 a year income from investments, or a $250,000 a year residual income?

The process for achieving each one is quite unique, so you will never know exactly what to do next to achieve your Dream Goal.

This is why you learned earlier that states of being, such as happiness or peace of mind, are not goals. There is no way for you to measure them and decide, in some objective manner, whether or not you've achieved them.

Can you imagine putting together a plan of action to "be happy" and saying, "Okay, I've taken steps one, two, and three; now I'm exactly 57 percent of the way to happiness"?

"If I just do these three things for the next 90 days, I'll be 92.4 percent of the way there and then by the end of the year, by golly, I'll be happy."

No! It just doesn't work that way. Happiness is a matter of choice. You can only be happy or have peace of mind if you choose to. You're either experiencing happiness or peace of mind, or you are not. As former U.S. President Abraham Lincoln once said, *"A man is just about as happy as he makes up his mind to be."*

Specific—Your Dream Goal must be *specific*. You need to know exactly what images to plant into your subconscious, so your mind and emotions can help you choose the actions that will lead to achieving it. Achieving your Dream Goal is no accident. It is done by deliberate, focused action.

To say, "I have become financially free," is not specific enough. Instead, say something like, "I have earned $1,000,000." That is quite specific and you can focus on achieving it.

You are designing your game of life here, so only put rules into it that guarantee you are going to win. Give yourself the best chance for success. Make your goal *Believable*, *Achievable*, *Measurable*, and *Specific*. In other words, give it some *BAMS*.

Goal-Achievement Step #4—*Make Sure Your Dream Goal Is Harmonious*
The final key to transforming your dream into a true goal is to make sure it's harmonious with the laws of nature and

your own beliefs and values. It wouldn't be in your best interest to spend your life going after goals that are either impossible to achieve, because they go against nature's laws, or can't be achieved without violating some of your most important beliefs and values.

<u>You now know all the keys for transforming your dream into a goal:</u>

1. Write it in present tense.
2. Give yourself a date for achieving it.
3. Make it believable, attainable, measurable, and specific.
4. And make it harmonious with the laws of nature and your beliefs and values.

Write Your Dream Goal Here:

_____

Checklist for Evaluating Your *Dream Goal:*

♦ Is my Dream Goal written in present tense?
♦ Have I chosen a date for achieving it?
♦ Have I given myself enough time, but not too much, to achieve it?
♦ Is my Dream Goal believable, achievable, measurable, and specific?
♦ Is my Dream Goal in harmony with natural laws?
♦ Is my Dream Goal in line with my beliefs and values?

If you've answered yes to all of the above questions, congratulations! It's now time to develop a plan.

Chapter 12

Become A *Goal Getter!*
Develop A Goal-Achievement Daily
Action Plan

"Plan tomorrow's work today."

Doing *Whatever It Takes*

A *Goal Getter* has a daily action plan and does whatever it takes to follow it. But, before we discuss how to develop your daily action plan, consider these ideas:

- ◆ You are directing your own life here. You're worth the time and effort it takes to be a champion and win at the game of life.

- ◆ Add up the hours you spent planning the last major project you worked on—maybe designing the addition to your home, having some friends over for dinner, or preparing for your daughter's wedding. You put in quite a bit of time and effort didn't you? And that was only for a tiny portion of your life. What you're doing now affects *the rest of your life.*

- ◆ The process you just completed is like the off season preparation a coach and his staff go through to get ready for next year. If you've ever been involved with athletics, you know a championship season is a year-round project. The coaches invest almost as much time and energy *preparing* for the season as they do coaching during the season.

Get ready to coach yourself for "Your Gold Medal Season" of goal-achievement. Here are six keys you can use to help you begin:

The Six Keys for Developing Your Goal-Achievement Daily (GAD) Action Plan

1. Let go of the past and forget any previous losses.
2. Sharpen your focus by eliminating distractions.
3. Shed the extra "weight" of false beliefs.
4. Overcome your fears by taking action.
5. Harness the hidden potential you were born with to help yourself succeed.
6. Develop your Goal-Achievement Daily Action Plan.

"GAD" Action Plan Key #1—*Let Go of the Past and Forget Any Previous Losses*

The first key is to let go of the past. Today is the first day of the rest of your life. It is a blank page and you can fill it with whatever you choose. As the designer of your own future, you are choosing success. Address these areas first:

♦ **The past does not determine your future unless you let it.** In the natural order of the world, your actions *today* determine the future you experience tomorrow. Since you are free to act and think any way you would like, *you are free to create any future you would like, no matter what happened in the past.* Just because you may have failed at something in the past does not mean you cannot succeed at it in the future!

From 1962 to 1968, the New York Mets had one of the poorest records ever recorded in the history of professional baseball. In fact, in 1968 the Mets finished ninth out of ten teams in the U.S. National League. Just one year later, they were sitting on top of the world after stunning the Baltimore Orioles in the World Series. You can turn your life around in the same way—when you commit to developing and carrying out a workable action plan.

♦ **What do you need to stop doing, even though you do it very well, in order to succeed at the particular goal you have chosen?** Let's say you're an excellent dentist, and you practice dentistry twelve to fifteen hours every day. Let's also say your Dream Goal is to retire from your practice by building another business. The first thing you need to do is give yourself time to do it.

Unless you have super-human energy and the ability to stay focused, you will be hard-pressed to also invest enough quality hours in building your other business—if you continue spending twelve to fifteen hours a day in dentistry. Therefore, even though you are excellent at it, you may want to consider hiring another dentist to help you with your patient load. Then you can invest more of your time and energy in the activities that are focused toward your Dream Goal. This is making the best use of your time.

Legend has it that an American singer, the late Frank Sinatra, was excellent at giving up the things that did not move him closer to his goal. One of my favorite sayings is "Frank Sinatra doesn't move pianos." This doesn't mean he was vain or thought he was too good to do manual labor. It just means he understood that his fame and fortune rested on his singing ability, not his ability to get the stage ready for him to sing! He did what he did best and allowed others to do what they did best. To move on most effectively you need to do the same.

♦ **What would a superstar do?** To determine what activities you need to do to maximize the time you invest in your Dream Goal, ask yourself, "What would a superstar do?" To be the best you can be in any given field of endeavor, duplicate what the most successful people in the field do.

The top performers in any arena do what they do, over and over again, before they become highly respected, successful leaders. Michael Jordan shot thousands of jump shots to become the world's best basketball player. Jack Nicklaus made thousands of chip shots, putts, and drives to take his golf game to a world-class level. Bill Gates invested thousands of hours in developing software and marketing strategies. This made Microsoft one of the world's most successful companies. And in the process, he became one of the world's wealthiest men.

These people are all world-class performers, but they were not born that way! They practiced the right activities relentlessly in order to take their games to the highest levels. They're "Goal Getters."

Do the same for your game. Do what the superstars do and you can become a Goal Getter too!

"GAD" Action Plan Key #2—*Sharpen Your Focus by Eliminating Distractions*

Once you have "cleaned your slate," by letting go of the past, you are ready to sharpen your focus on your Dream Goal—by eliminating distractions from your life. In the case of goal-achieving, any activity that doesn't move you closer to your Dream Goal is a distraction you need to postpone or eliminate.

For example, if your Dream Goal is to win an Olympic gold medal, winning the Nobel Prize is a distraction. If your Dream Goal is to build a successful business, coaching your child's soccer team is a distraction.

What are your weekly activities? Which contribute directly to your Dream Goal? Which do not? Continue doing those things that contribute directly to achieving your Dream Goal and eliminate everything else that does not.

"GAD" Action Plan Key #3—*Shed The Extra "Weight" of False Beliefs*

It's likely that some, or perhaps even many, of the beliefs you hold don't support your efforts in achieving your Dream Goal. In fact, these beliefs actually work against you. Keeping these beliefs is like lugging a "spare tire" around your middle. They slow you down and keep you from performing at your best. You need to get rid of them in order to allow yourself to move more smoothly to world class goal-getter status. In that process, you adopt thinking based on solid success principles.

Since we already covered many of the limiting beliefs and paradigms most people seem to have, I won't repeat them. However, you may need to go back to your list of core beliefs and carefully think about each of them. Does each belief contribute to the achievement of your Dream Goal or does it hold you back?

Get rid of beliefs that hold you back and replace them with new, more productive beliefs. Beliefs are like habits. Eliminate old beliefs by replacing them with new ones that become success habits.

"GAD" Action Plan Key #4—*Overcome Your Fears by Taking Action*

Whenever someone decides to move on, it's not at all uncommon for them to feel a sense of fear deep down inside—a feeling of uncertainty, that they're not so sure they *can* make the necessary changes in their life. Some may also feel they're not too sure they *want* to invest all the time and energy required to turn their dreams into reality.

If you feel that way too, that's okay—it's normal. After all, you're growing. Growth involves stepping boldly into the unknown, which is often a bit scary. If you *didn't* feel that way, you'd have a right to be concerned because it may mean you aren't growing. So, let's go back to those feelings of doubt or fear that you may have. To help yourself overcome them, remember these four points:

1. Fear is a sign you're growing!
2. We learn our fears—so we can unlearn them.
3. You need to release the old to make room for the new.
4. Those people you are closest to often want you to keep your fears.

"Fear and doubt knocked on the door. Faith and courage answered. There was no one there."
Old proverb

"Fear is holding a mental picture of what you don't want to happen."
Lewis Timberlake

Overcoming Fear Point #1—*Fear is a sign you're growing!* If you don't feel fear on a daily basis, you're undoubtedly in your comfort zone! And remember, it's impossible to grow if you stay in your comfort zone all the time. Rejoice in your fear because it is a healthy response from your body telling you that you're growing.

Fear comes when the thoughts and images you are placing into your subconscious are new to the beliefs that are already there. Every time you feel your fear, just tell yourself, "I understand I am feeling fear because the new thoughts I am having are creating a conflict in my subconscious. This is alright. It means I am re-programming my subconscious and growing into using more of my potential as a human being who's winning more at the game of life!"

Overcoming Fear Point #2—*We learn our fears—so we can unlearn them.* *Fears are conditioned responses to your* *environment. You were born practically fearless.* The only fears most of us are born with are the fear of falling and fear of loud noises. Virtually every additional fear develops later as a response to the events in your life. The root of all your fears is simply the belief that you can't handle whatever life may bring you.

To diminish your fears, start telling yourself you can handle whatever comes your way! Since you learned most of your fears as a product of your conditioning, you have the capability to *unlearn* them as well. You can start by asking yourself the following questions:

- ◆ Why do I believe I can't do this thing?
- ◆ Is there a rational reason for this belief?
- ◆ Could I be mistaken in this belief?
- ◆ Why do I continue to act and feel this fear?
- ◆ What is the worst thing that could happen to me if I went ahead and did the thing I am afraid of doing?

View this as a process of discovery. You are discovering why you think and act the way you do. You are discovering more about yourself and the world around you. You are discovering just how much fun it can be to test those limits and overcome your fears.

Overcoming Fear Point #3—*You need to release the old to make room for the new.* Which would motivate you more: the chance to earn $100,000 in the next year or the opportunity, or necessity, to keep from losing the $100,000 you earned last year? Most people would say they'd be more motivated to work to keep from losing the $100,000 they already had than to gain the $100,000 they hadn't yet earned. For most of us, the fear of loss is stronger than the potential for gain. Is that true for you?

If you live your life believing this, you will minimize your growth. You'll tie up virtually all your energy trying to hold on to the things you think you already have. This thinking doesn't work for two reasons:

First, you don't really "own" physical things because they are all temporary. Trying to hold on to them is like trying to run in quicksand. You'll just sink in deeper, and never feel very secure inside if you try to do it.

Second, if you're spending your time and energy holding on to what you already have—material things, belief systems, relationships, and all the rest—you won't have a whole lot of time or energy left for pursuing what you really want.

Think about that for a minute. If you're just trying to hold on to what you already have, you're guaranteeing that you'll never get what you really want. You need to let go of one to get the other.

Think of this process as a "spring cleaning." Say you want some new clothes but your closet is still full of old ones. Until you clean out the closet and get rid of the clothes you don't need anymore, you won't have any room for the new ones. Makes sense, doesn't it?

Begin your own spring cleaning. Begin letting go of all the things in your life that are holding you back. Let go of your limiting values and beliefs, and the physical possessions that aren't totally ideal for you. Make room for the new. Get ready for the burst of energy you'll feel as you free up your resources by releasing the old!

Overcoming Fear Point #4—*Those people you are closest to often want you to keep your fears.* Frequently, the people you're closest to will try to sabotage your dreams and help you keep your fears. They try to come across as though they were protecting you. They may simply be afraid that if you overcome your fears and succeed, you'll move on and leave them behind. They don't want to "lose" you so they may try to hold you back in an attempt to keep you from getting ahead of them. If that is so, it is, of course, a sad situation for them. They just may be jealous of you! But don't let that concern you.

The best thing you can do for yourself, and them, is to become a shining example. Be a growing human being who is overcoming fears daily and realizing more and more of the potential you have inside.

These people do not need you and they will not lose you—there's no way they can possess you to begin with! Just thank them for their "concern" and move on with your life. Tell them that if they won't encourage you to at least not discourage you.

And if someone is downright negative, you may want to consider staying away from them.

Associate with others, like yourself, who are moving on and working toward their dreams. Hang around positive thinking people. Read positive books and listen to positive tapes to help you stay on track.

The people who truly care about you will respect you and your decision to move on. And, if you keep an open-minded, loving attitude toward them, they'll realize you still care about them. In fact, they may eventually begin to follow your lead down the path of growth.

"GAD" Action Plan Key #5—*Harness the hidden potential you were born with to help yourself succeed.*

It's now time for you to use what author Earl Nightingale called "The Strangest Secret"—the incredible power of your subconscious mind. This is one of the most powerful ways to stay focused on achieving your goals.

In order to get "The Strangest Secret" to work for you, you need to follow these three steps:

1. Picture your Dream Goal in the present—"as if" you've already made it happen.
2. Solidify your image of your Dream Goal in your mind.

3. Turn this mental image, of you having already achieved your Dream Goal, over to your subconscious mind and let it help you make your goal a reality.

"Strangest Secret" Step #1—*Picture your Dream Goal in the present, as if you've already made it happen.* We've already discussed the importance of thinking of your goal in the present tense, as if you've already achieved it. As you know, your mind deals only with the present—it doesn't recognize past or future tense. Imagining yourself in possession of your Dream Goal in the present strengthens the connection between your conscious mind, your subconscious mind and your body. It also allows all of the resources at your command to begin working together.

Start practicing this now. Sit down and be still. Gently relax all your muscles. Let your abdomen sag and your jaw drop. Close your eyes and let your imagination run free. Keep picturing your Dream Goal so vividly that your subconscious accepts it as a part of you and you'll be driven to take action.

What does it feel like to have achieved your Dream Goal? What do you look like standing in possession of it? What are the sights, sounds and smells around you? What emotions are you experiencing? Who else is in the picture? What do they think of you? What do they do to congratulate you on achieving your Dream Goal?

To make this process easier and more effective, get a symbol to represent your Dream Goal. One of the best ways to do this is to have someone take a picture of you with it. If your Dream Goal is a new Cadillac, go down to your local dealership. Ask the sales person to snap a couple of photos of you sitting in the car or standing happily next to it. Then go take it for a test drive. If your Dream Goal is a new house, find one you would like and have someone take a picture of you standing in front of it.

If your Dream Goal is to travel to Italy, go to your local travel agent and get a big poster with a scene from Italy that you want to visit. Have your picture taken in front of the poster, so it puts you "in the picture."

If your Dream Goal is to become a leader in your business or profession, you may want to picture yourself being recognized for your achievements at a seminar or dinner meeting. You could call your local high school and ask if you could have a friend take some pictures of you standing on their auditorium stage.

You could then dress up in your best clothing and pose on stage as if you were receiving an award. You could also pose at the podium with the microphone, as if you were telling your story, inspiring others to let them know they can do it, too!

You could also picture yourself as a new leader, at some resort location with the leaders you've always admired. Then you could take a photo of you, or you with your leader, and glue it on to the picture.

It's also easy to scan a photo of you and a photo of your Dream Goal, and then merge them in the computer so they can be printed out as a full-color composite picture. If you or a friend has a computer with a scanner, you may want to do this. Looking at this picture could have a real positive effect on you!

Another excellent symbol of your Dream Goal is a goal card. Use the blank side of a business card or cut some paper into that size. Write your Dream Goal on the card or paper and always carry it with you. It may even be more effective to put a picture of you with your Dream Goal on one side of the card and the written description of it on the other. Look at it often as you go through the day.

Here's another excellent idea. If your Dream Goal is to earn a certain amount of money, go down to the bank and get a blank check register book or use one you have at home that you don't need. Record your weekly or monthly "deposits" from the income you will be earning and record your "net balance" at the end of your goal-achievement period.

For example, if your goal is to earn $100,000 in one year, record a deposit of $8,333.33 on the last day of each month. Increase your balance each month until it reaches $100,000 the twelfth month. You can do the same thing with a few blank tax returns. Change the date on the return to the appropriate year and record the income you will earn that year.

Whatever symbol you choose, display it prominently where you'll see it on a regular basis. You may even want to get copies made and place one in your office, one on the dashboard of your car, one on the refrigerator, one in your bathroom, and one near your bed.

The idea is to keep building a clearer and clearer picture of yourself in possession of or having accomplished your dream Goal. The pictures will help you do that. When you keep something in sight, it will also be on your mind—*within sight, within mind.*

Your *Dreambuilding Book* Revisited

Take a few minutes now and insert pages in your *Dreambuilding Book* for each of the aspects of your overall dream. Add the picture of you in possession of your Dream Goal, a written description of it, and pictures of other things you would like to do, see, or experience. Also include people you would like to meet, your personal creed, core beliefs, your mission or focus statement, and anything else you would like to include.

"Strangest Secret" Step #2—*Solidify your image of your Dream Goal in your mind.* Picturing your Dream Goal in the present and having a symbol to represent it gives you something basic to work with. The next step is to turn that picture into a "blueprint" for a bridge between where you are now and where you want to be. Solidifying the picture is like building a bridge from your blueprint. The better the blueprint, the better bridge you'll build—and the easier and quicker you can achieve your Dream Goal.

You've already engaged the power of your eyes and the written word in this process. Now add the power of the spoken word.

Get a blank audiocassette tape and record your written description of your Dream Goal, in your own voice. Use personal pronouns (I, we, me, and us rather than you), speak in the present tense, and make your description short and specific. For example, you could say: "My family and I are now living in our beautiful dream home, located high on a hill overlooking the city. We are driving our dream cars, and we just took delivery of a motorcoach. Best of all, we are happy and debt free. I'm now a leader in my field, with a business that spans the globe."

Next, record a description of what it feels like to have achieved your Dream Goal—the sights, sounds, smells, and emotions that you're experiencing. Make your descriptions as vivid and real sounding as possible.

You could clearly describe being on a stage, getting recognized for your accomplishments, and sharing your story with the audience. You could also detail your first trip to a leadership conference as a new high-level producer "as if" you are now there. Describe whatever your picture is of your Dream Goal like moving into your dream house, "as if" it's happening as you're talking.

Imagine you are an award-winning actor or actress portraying yourself in the screenplay of your life. Get into the role whole-heartedly. Laugh, yell, cry, giggle, or whatever seems appropriate to really describe your Dream Goal. You could say, "I'm here in my shorts relaxing on a chaise lounge under an enormous palm tree, drinking a cold, refreshing glass of iced tea. I'm celebrating going to a new leadership level, here at this magnificently lush resort. In the lounge chairs next to me are my leaders and mentors.

"Believe it or not, the president of the corporation just gave us a big smile as they walked by in their colorful shirt with tropical fruits on it and white shorts. What a tan! They look like they've been here a lot.

"Three other leaders just walked by. Wow, here comes the photographer wearing a straw hat and bright green and purple clothes! He just snapped a picture of us to go in our company's monthly publication. It's really happening! A bunch of us are heading out now to go snorkeling in the warm, aqua-colored water. It's so clear I can see the bottom of the lagoon. There go a couple more leaders with their tennis rackets walking to the courts on the other side of the big sparkling fountains. This is incredible—becoming a leader and spending time with these other leaders whom I respect and admire so much. They're my heroes. What a great trip! I think I'll play a round of golf tomorrow."

You may even want to play some inspirational music in the background. Some examples would be the theme from a movie like *Rocky*, the *William Tell Overture* or the title song from the movie *Top Gun*. This will help stir your soul and make your dreams more vivid.

The point is, you need to get emotionally involved with your Dream Goal to help you bring out more of your potential. Recording your goal in this manner helps you develop an intense emotional desire to achieve it. This helps solidify in your mind the picture of you already living your dream.

"Strangest Secret" Step #3—*Turn your mental picture of you having achieved your Dream Goal over to your subconscious mind and let it help you make it happen.* You've now developed a picture of you in possession of the Dream Goal you've set. You have consciously thought about it, and you've used your sight and hearing to help solidify this mental image on a conscious level.

Now it's time to use "The Strangest Secret"—the power of your subconscious mind. With it, you'll be driven to *attract* to yourself the resources and circumstances necessary to achieve your Dream Goal.

To use the power of your subconscious, you need to turn your perfected picture of your Dream Goal over to it and enlist its support for your cause. You've completed the *first step* of this process by making written, visual, and verbal descriptions of this goal.

The *second step* is to relax and consciously imagine yourself having achieved your Dream Goal. This will allow you to benefit from "The Great Secret Of Success."

The Great Secret of Success

As mentioned briefly in Chapter Two, you could think of your subconscious as the hard drive of a computer. Inside are "programmed" all the thoughts and ideas that form the basis of the habits you live by. To get a new thought or idea into your "hard drive" you need to turn on your "computer" and convince yourself, through positive self-talk, to load in some new "software." The more you say what you want and the more emotion you say it with, the more likely you are to convince yourself to load the new "software." Once you do, the new thoughts or ideas are "installed" and now reside in your "hard drive"—your subconscious!

Continually picturing yourself having achieved your goal is equivalent to presenting your new thoughts and ideas to your subconscious over and over again. Do this enough, with emotion, and your subconscious will accept it. The new thoughts and ideas are now a part of you and form the basis of new habits for you to live by, so you can achieve your Dream Goal.

"GAD" Action Plan Key #6—*Develop Your Goal-Achievement Daily Action Plan*

To develop a simple, yet powerful plan for achieving your Dream Goal, answer these questions:

♦ What 3-6 actions, when done daily, will move you the furthest and quickest toward your Dream Goal?
♦ What is the *first step* you need to take to reach your Dream Goal?
♦ What are the *next steps?*
♦ What are the *milestones* that will tell you you're on the right track?
♦ What *rewards* will you receive along the way?
♦ *Who will you be accountable* to for the actions you need to take to achieve your Dream Goal?
♦ How will you schedule your time for maximum Dream Goal achievement effectiveness?

Those questions may sound simple, but they're extremely important. This is the area where most would-be goal-achievers fall short. They go through all this work to set their goals, then they rush out to "set the world on fire."

The problem is, they failed to develop an *effective plan.* Therefore, they soon become frustrated from their lack of progress. Or they're confused because they seemed incredibly busy for the past few months and yet they didn't move any closer to their Dream Goal. They were indeed busy. Yet, without a plan of action, they weren't productive. Similar to the hamster running in his circular cage—they were going nowhere fast.

So, let's examine each of these questions in more depth so you don't make the same mistakes.

What 3-6 Actions, When Done Daily, Will Move You the Furthest and Quickest Toward Achieving Your Dream Goal? What Are Your Goal-Achievement Daily Activities?

What you're looking for here are the important, but not necessarily urgent, activities.

A good example is someone in sales who sets a goal to earn $100,000 in commissions a year, or about double what he did the previous year. His critical daily actions were: contacting at least 10 new prospects, making enough phone calls to schedule two appointments, and investing 10-15 minutes planning tomorrow's activities. He knew that by disciplining himself to do these things consistently, every day, for a certain period of time, he would make enough sales to achieve his Dream Goal.

Here are a few more examples of the potential Goal-Achievement Daily Activities for different types of goals:

Conventional Entrepreneurial Activities: Sending samples to 10 new potential customers, contacting 3 other suppliers for quotations, investing one hour in walking the shop floor to talk to employees, investing one hour in reading relevant trade journals and personal development books, or investing an hour in training employees.

Athletic Activities: Running 5 miles, shooting 100 free throws, making 100 putts, hitting 100 pitches, or investing one hour in lifting weights.

Health Activities: Eating less than 20 percent of your calories from fat, eating less than 2,000 calories a day, eating at least 5 servings of fruits and vegetables, and working out for a least 30 minutes.

Personal Activities: Investing one hour in quality time with your family, telling your spouse and kids you love them at least once, sincerely complimenting at least one of your friends or family members, and listening to your spouse share their feelings for at least 30 minutes.

Notice a couple of things about these examples:

1. They're simple.
2. They're tasks that move you toward your Dream Goal in the quickest manner possible.
3. They're specific and measurable.

You are looking for the few key areas to focus on that will catapult you toward your Dream Goal. Usually these areas are very easy to understand and simple to accomplish. A golfer knows that when he sinks 100 putts a day, he'll lower his overall score. Sales people know that when they contact 10 prospects a day, they'll sell more products. Parents know that when they invest one hour each day in listening to their kids share their thoughts, they'll develop better relationships with them.

The key thing here is that you're focusing your time and energy doing the things that'll move you toward your Dream Goal as quickly as possible. It's likely you may realize three things when you are thinking about the key actions you need to take to achieve your Dream Goal:

1. These tasks may or may not be what you do well. Don't be afraid to admit that what you do well may not be the most important thing for achieving your Dream Goal. You could be one of the best in your current occupation but that may not help you much if your Dream Goal is to be financially free. That's okay. For example, you were inexperienced at your career when you originally chose it.

By doing the important things daily, no matter what, you will become better at them. It's just like lifting weights. The more you lift, the easier it is for your muscles to move the weights. Sometimes, though, it requires some humility to learn new skills—especially when you're accustomed to being one of the best in your occupation.

2. The tasks may or may not be what you usually do. For instance, you may be used to operating a computer all day long. However, if you want to be a million-dollar producer, you'll probably have to do something else. You may find that one of the key actions you need to take is to meet and talk to three or more new people every day. Your new goal will probably require doing some things you aren't used to doing and that you may not initially be good at. You may, at first, feel uncomfortable as you stretch outside your comfort zone...and that's okay. Do these things anyway.

You overcome fear by taking action. You build skills by taking action. You grow through taking action. You're like water in a pond. Without any action, you stagnate. By taking action, your entire environment comes alive with new growth and prosperity which, like moving water, helps the pond's ecosystem grow and prosper.

3. The tasks must be specific and measurable. You must be able to tell if and when you've completed your daily tasks. It does you absolutely no good to say, "I will talk to some new prospects today." Does that mean talking to one—or one dozen? Nebulous goals give you little, if any, results. Specific, measurable goals give you "a track to run on"—*something to make yourself accountable for.*

What will it take to help you reach the level of performance you want and need, to accomplish your Dream Goal? The key in this whole process is not coming up with some convoluted, complicated plan. Rather, it's picking a handful of truly important things and doing them, day in and day out, no matter what. No exceptions, no excuses!

By doing *whatever it takes*, you show you're serious about achieving your Dream Goal—not just talking about it.

Now that you've decided on your Goal-Achievement Daily Activities ask yourself, "If I complete these activities each day, can I *be sure* I will achieve my Dream Goal?"

If you answered no, go back and revise them until you can answer yes. Once you can honestly answer yes, copy them onto a clean sheet of paper with the heading "My Dream Goal Daily Activities: I am committed to taking these actions every day, before I go to bed. No excuse! I'm doing it." Add these to your *Dreambuilding Book*. And record them, in your own voice, on the goal-achievement audiocassette you made earlier.

◆ What's the First Step?

The next question you need to answer to complete your Goal-Achievement Daily Action Plan is: "What is the first step toward my Dream Goal?"

By this time, the first step you need to take is probably clear to you. If it's not, begin with a picture of you having achieved your Dream Goal and work backward.

What must have occurred right before you achieved your Dream Goal? What must have occurred right before that? And right before that? Eventually, you will work your way back to the first step you need to take.

You won't always be able to determine every single step from where you are now to where you want to be. In fact, you will typically have areas where you can only guess at what must occur. That's another good reason for you to have a big dream—it will cause you to stretch your imagination and grow into the person you need to be to achieve it.

Don't let the fact that you don't know every step in advance keep you from getting started. The key is to figure out what the first step is, and leave it at that. Once you complete the first step, you'll be able to see what you need to do next.

As writer Thomas Carlyle once said, *"Go as far as you can see. When you get there, you'll see how to go farther."*

◆ What Do You Think the Next Step Is?

The next element of your Goal-Achievement Daily Action Plan is to determine what you *think* the next step is. Notice I said "think."

The funny thing about setting and achieving lofty goals—the kind that make you stretch—is that you'll never know all the steps you need to take in advance! Long-term planning never works exactly the way you want it to because there are so many variables in life. But it's still valuable to plan so you can give yourself a general direction to move in. Invest as much time as you need mapping out what you think the next step is to achieve your goal.

Then outline all the subsequent steps you think will be necessary to reach your goal. Remember, *how* you are going to accomplish these steps is irrelevant at this point. As former U.S. President Abraham Lincoln once said, *"Always bear in mind your own resolution to succeed is more important than any one other thing."*

◆ What Are the Milestones That Will Tell You Whether You're On Track?

Now that you have a tentative plan for achieving your Dream Goal, it's time to set up milestones, which will help you stay on track. Think of your milestones as road markers. They tell you how many miles it is to your destination. They also tell you how many miles you've come since you started your journey of success. It's important to give yourself credit for how far you've come—especially when you're hurdling obstacles along the way.

Break your Dream Goal down into 3-10 manageable chunks or smaller goals. Then set milestones that will tell you when you're due to reach them. If your Dream Goal is money-related, you may want to set milestones at certain percentages of the goal. For example, if your Dream Goal is to earn $100,000 in annual income—your milestones may be $10,000, $25,000, $50,000 and $75,000.

◆ What Rewards Will You Receive Along the Way?

One of the most important parts of goal-achieving is enjoying the journey. If you give up all your present-moment pleasure for some elusive future vision of the "utopia" you will live in when you achieve your goal, you will never be happy. Even if you do achieve your Dream Goal, you will feel a fleeting bit of pleasure and then you will be empty inside once again. You need to live your life as fully as possible along the line. Sure you'll need to sacrifice some things. But you don't need to sacrifice everything you enjoy.

Take time to "smell the roses" by setting up a series of rewards for yourself as you reach each milestone on the way to your goal. These rewards need to be meaningful only to you as you accomplish things along the way.

For instance, treat yourself to an ice cream sundae, or something else you enjoy, when you have made five presentations in one week. Use a lunch break to test drive your dream car in celebration of making your first $1,000 bonus check. Or enjoy a romantic dinner with your spouse when you reach a certain volume of business or sales.

♦ How Will You Invest Your Time for Maximum Goal Achievement?

Now you know what you need to do and who you will be accountable to for doing it. Next, you need to develop a plan for actually doing it on a daily basis. You probably have your own method of accomplishing your Goal-Achievement Daily Activities, but the following 11 keys will give you some important guidelines to follow:

♦ **"GAD" Activities Key #1—*Do the important, not the "urgent," things first. Schedule your most important Goal-Achievement Daily Activities the night before.*** This gives you "a track to run on," reducing the temptation to procrastinate. Don't be concerned about doing the so-called "urgent" things, like mowing the grass, that someone else can do, or you could do later as time permits. Don't let "urgent" things keep you from doing the important things.

♦ **"GAD" Activities Key #2—*Block periods of the day for a specific priority.*** One powerful way to do this is to divide your week into 21 even blocks. Each day will have three blocks: morning, afternoon, and evening. Make a chart with these 21 blocks on it. Then fill in the general priority you will address during each period.

For example, first check your yearly and monthly schedule of seminars and other business-related activities.

Plug these into your schedule so you can plan for and around them.

One of your general activities in the morning block each day may be to meet someone new. This could be done at a local restaurant where you eat breakfast or just stop in for coffee on your way to work.

You can then list the people you'll follow up on next week. Or, your general priority activity for the afternoon or evening blocks may be giving at least one presentation each day.

Allow some time for relaxation and rejuvenation. Use it to renew your energy—quiet time to think, review your goals and do some planning, take a nap, or put your feet up and read something you enjoy. It's also helpful to schedule one block, perhaps Saturday or Sunday afternoon, for "catch up" to do all the little tasks you haven't done the rest of the week. And be sure to allow at least 15 to 20 minutes every day for your personal development reading and time to listen to at least one continuing education tape a day. Make wise use of your time by playing these tapes while you're getting ready for work, driving your car, and getting ready for bed.

"Blocking" your time in this way simplifies your life and makes it easier to plan your goal-achievement program. The principle here is to organize weekly and then adapt daily. If 21 blocks doesn't work for you, you may want to add an extra block each day around lunch or dinnertime. This would be a good way to build some exercise time into your program. You could walk at lunch every day and listen to a positive tape as you go.

Once you have your general blocks filled in, don't change them. The basic rule to remember is, work when you work, play when you play, and don't mix the two. If you're in a "prospecting" block, do nothing but prospect. If you are in a "family time" block, do nothing but spend time with your family. And enjoy the time wholeheartedly, without guilt. This is part of your plan for living a happy, productive, well-balanced life.

♦ **"GAD" Activities Key #3—***Decide on your highest priorities and have the courage to say no to everything that doesn't support them.* In your blocks, you've scheduled your priorities. If someone asks you to do something that does not match your priorities, politely decline their invitation and move forward on your goal-achieving activities. If something comes up that doesn't support your highest values, or doesn't contribute directly to your Dream Goal, don't do it.

Many of us complain that there aren't enough hours in the day to get everything done that we need to do. The truth is, *we all have all the time there is,* and we all choose how to spend or invest it Make wise time and energy investments, and make each day count.

Choose goal-achieving activities. Decline tension-relieving activities such as watching television, or exchanging gossip with the neighbors. To make these decisions about what to do, ask yourself, *"In five years, doing which of these activities will affect my life in the most positive manner?"* Then do it—joyously and guiltlessly.

♦ **"GAD" Activities Key #4—***Become "ambitiously lazy."* You probably thought all this goal-achieving stuff was hard work, didn't you? Now's your chance to become lazy—ambitiously lazy—without remorse or guilt. *Become ambitiously lazy at doing anything that does not contribute to living your dream.*

Say you have some things you think you "should" be doing right now, but doing them wouldn't contribute to your achieving your dream. Get lazy. Don't do them. It's likely that, in a day or so, you'll realize they weren't important enough to do anyway. Besides which, a lot of issues tend to resolve themselves if we just give them some time. And for goodness sake, don't try to make everything perfect, because it can't be done! Strive for excellence instead.

♦ **"GAD" Activities Key #5—***Delegate, delegate, delegate.* Before doing something ask yourself, "Is doing this the best use of my time?" Say you've got some things that must be done. But you know it wouldn't be the wisest choice for you to spend your valuable time doing them. As long as someone else can do them—delegate them.

What's your time worth? With each person you meet, you could potentially be starting a life-long friendship or a business relationship. With every seminar you attend, you could be gaining the motivation, inspiration and knowledge to take you to your next level of accomplishment. For example isn't it worth it to hire a teenager to baby-sit, so you invest more of your time and energy in your financial future? Only you can answer that.

♦ **"GAD" Activities Key #6—***To do more, believe more in your potential.* That's why we've focused so much on understanding yourself and the laws of nature. By increasing your knowledge and understanding, you're becoming more aware of your hidden talents and abilities. Your awareness of them builds belief, which increases your self-confidence, enabling you to better express them. As you do, you can accomplish more in less time. And the bonus is, the more you do, the more you grow and become.

♦ **"GAD" Activities Key #7—***Just do it.* This old Nike slogan was used to sell shoes and it's also a great motto for life. *Rather than looking for ways to do things, just do them.*

♦ **"GAD" Activities Key #8—***Be aware of the appropriateness of the things you're doing.* Once you're aware that you're doing things that don't contribute to achieving your goals, you'll realize there's an alternative. Focus on your most important daily tasks. Simplifying your life through "blocking" your days, will allow you to establish a pattern of productive well-paced work.

American essayist, Henry David Thoreau once said, *"As he simplifies his life, the laws of nature will become less complex."* Your 100 percent focus on the activity at hand could help you get twice as much done in half the time. Your energy won't be drained by negative emotions and distracting, non-goal-achieving thoughts and activities.

♦ **"GAD" Activities Key #9—***Don't start your day until you have it "finished."* If you start your day not knowing exactly what you plan to accomplish, you probably won't get much of anything done. "Don't start your day until you have it finished" means, *plan tomorrow's work today.* Invest five or ten minutes at the end of each day outlining and prioritizing, preferably in your day planner, what you plan to accomplish the next day. This serves two important purposes:

First, you'll save time by immediately going to work on the most important tasks, first thing in the morning. Second, by planning tomorrow today, you're placing the thoughts of what you want to accomplish into your subconscious. You're giving it the entire night to go to work to help you become aware of the best way to accomplish these things. Always keep your planner by your bed so you can record these ideas, whenever they come to you.

♦ **"GAD" Activities Key #10—***The more you dare to do, the more you can do.* Increase your accomplishments by reaching just beyond your current capabilities. Imagine yourself as a gymnast who wants to do the splits. Each day you stretch a little more than the day before. You pull your muscles to the point where they begin to strain, and then hold them there. Gradually, you relax the muscles knowing they're getting more flexible every day. Soon, you're able to drop into the splits quickly and effortlessly.

♦ **"GAD" Activities Key #11—***Risk to be free.* Do what's in your heart; it was meant just for you. Adopt the "ready, fire, aim" philosophy. Do things and make adjustments as you go. You can do it. Don't concern yourself about what other people may say. It doesn't matter. They're not paying your bills, they don't know what you're feeling, and they can't live your life for you. Here's an inspirational quote that may help you:

Risk To Be Free

To laugh is to risk appearing a fool.
To weep is to risk appearing sentimental.
To reach out for another is to risk
exposing your true self.
To place your ideas, your dreams before
the crowd is to risk their loss.
To love is to risk not being loved in return.
To live is to risk dying.
To hope is to risk despair. To try is to risk failure.
But risks need to be taken because
the greatest hazard in life is to risk nothing.
The person who risks nothing does
nothing, has nothing, is nothing.
He may avoid suffering and sorrow,
but he simply cannot learn, feel,
change, grow, love...live.
Chained by his beliefs, he is a slave;
he has forfeited freedom.
Only a person who risks is free.

Chapter 13

Make It Happen And Enjoy The Results

"You don't just luck into things... You build step-by-step, whether it's friendships or opportunities."
Barbara Bush

Go For It!

You now have an incredibly powerful game plan for achieving your goals without giving up your life. All that's left is for you to execute your plan, fine tune it for maximum results, and enjoy the journey toward living your dream.

Take Action Daily Toward Your Dream Goal

Executing your game plan is a simple process. It involves only four main steps:

♦ At the end of each day, or before you go to bed, complete your Goal-Achievement Daily Action Plan for the next day.

♦ When you reach one milestone, determine what your next step is and keep moving forward—staying focused on your Dream Goal.

♦ Repeat the process until you reach your Dream Goal.

♦ Dream bigger and set another Dream Goal, using this process to achieve it.

That's basically all there is to it. The key here is *consistency*—keep doing the right things long enough, and you *will* achieve your Dream Goal. As noted author Viktor Frankl once said, *"Man does not simply exist, but always decides what his existence will be, what he will become in the next moment."*

Refine Your Actions So You Can Achieve Your Goals More Quickly

Sporting events are won and lost by minuscule amounts. The difference between a person who wins and a person who loses is often hundredths of a second or fractions of a percent! Some people call this *the razor's edge*.

The difference between Mark McGwire, who hit 70 homeruns, more than anyone else in baseball history, and Sammy Sosa, who is the number two with 66, is only one more homerun every forty games. That's it. Only one homerun every forty games makes the difference between baseball's all-time best homerun hitter and the guy who came in second. That's a difference of only 2.5 percent!

The difference between a World Series ring and a last-place finish is usually about one extra victory per week. That's it. Instead of being stretched out on the couch in your living room after suffering through an also-ran season, you're celebrating a world championship in October.

And, the difference between multi-billionaire Warren Buffett, arguably the world's most successful investor, and everyone else is only about 1.5 percent per month! After 35 years of earning 1.5 percent per month extra (*the razor's edge*) a $1,000 investment turns into an extra $36 million if your annual returns were 35 percent instead of 17 percent.

Your goal is to give yourself *the razor's edge*. This is what helps superstar baseball players get that one additional hit every five games. It then helps their team to win one more game per week, giving them the championship. And it's what can propel you into a super-star leader in your business or profession.

In order to develop that *razor's edge* which separates the champions from the rest of the pack, you need to do three things:

1. Build your belief.
2. Build your desire.
3. Model yourself after other champions.

Harness the twin powers of belief and desire, and model yourself after successful people. Develop *the razor's edge* that separates the winners from the whiners.

Build Your Belief and Trust in the Power of Your Dream

Building your belief is the first step in developing the *razor's edge* in your goal-achievement plan. You can achieve your goals only when you believe you can do it. As Henry Ford once said, "Think you can, think you can't; either way, you'll be right." And the *Bible* tells us, "All things whatsoever ye ask in prayer, *believing,* ye shall receive."

By understanding how your incredible mind works, your values, and your role in the world, you can develop an unshakable belief in your ability to achieve your goals. It's easy to believe in the things you can see and touch—that's what average-thinking people do. But, *the most successful people are visionary—they also believe in those things they cannot see and touch.* This comes from having faith in their dream, which helps them turn it into reality.

The best test of your belief is how you act on an everyday basis. *Do you prepare to succeed or prepare to fail?* You can accomplish only what you expect. When you expect success and act like you have success, you will continue to receive success. If you expect failure and prepare for failure, you'll get failure. *We can shape the way things can be because we tend to act according to our expectations.*

If you are going to doubt something, doubt your limits, not your abilities. When you build your faith and belief, follow your game plan, and do whatever it takes, you cannot help but realize your goals!

Whatever mental picture, backed by faith, you hold of your dream, your subconscious—your ever-dutiful "servant" —will help you bring to pass. Close your eyes, relax, and visualize yourself living your dream. Feel the emotions. Believe in your abilities. Trust the power of your dream.

The Power of True, Strong Desire

The next key component of turning your thoughts into dreams is *desire*. Your desire wields a power as strong as your belief in turning your thoughts into things. *You can believe something all you want, but it's only when you fuel it with the power of your desire that you can turn it into reality.* Sometimes you'll accomplish a goal or make a smaller dream come true with a little belief and desire. But those times will be few and far between. Only strong desire backing your belief will enable you to accomplish a Dream Goal that requires consistent, focused action over a long period of time.

Harnessing the power of your desire gives you the certainty to predict that what you truly want will come into your life. Think of your desires as arising from the potential inside of you. Knowing this is simply your capacity for success, your true desires can be fulfilled. You may have a wish or a thought that's not fulfilled, but you'll never have a burning desire that cannot be fulfilled.

How do you distinguish whether your desire is burning or not? A burning desire is one you get emotionally involved with. It's one that really "fires you up," not just for a few hours or a few days, but for the long-term. It's one that you get excited thinking about when you're all alone. You're pumped up and internally motivated by your true burning desire. External motivation just serves to reinforce your heartfelt passion, which comes from deep inside. You sense its realization will be an expression of your unique talents and potential. "You know that you know that you know" this is something you were meant to accomplish. As Robert Browning once said, *"Our aspirations are our possibilities."*

Most importantly, a true desire is one in which *you take action* to make it come true. Doing whatever it takes to make it happen is worth it to you. You can sit around all day and dream about having a new luxury car, for example, but that's all it is—a daydream. Having a new Cadillac or other luxury car, becomes a true burning desire when you get emotionally involved in it. It's when you can see, hear, and feel yourself in your dream car smoothly cruising down the road with your favorite music on the stereo—*before* you ever own it. When you are committed to investing a minimum of several hours every week consistently taking actions leading to the fulfillment of your desire, you'll get it. It'll just be a matter of time before it happens.

If you don't get emotionally involved with your desire and aren't willing to take action to turn it into reality, it's not a true burning desire. It is a wish—a daydream.

Your desire helps you to focus your mind, like a laser beam, on one goal. It focuses the images of the dream being formed in your subconscious mind. All the power you have is working together to help you do what is necessary for you to realize your desire. *Once you have a true burning desire, you'll feel focused and clear about your objective.*

How Can You Build Your Desire?

As you focus, you'll doggedly overcome any obstacles that get in your way. You're going forward in faith knowing that the precise direction and exactly what you need to do will become evident as you go. In the face of any challenges, your true burning desire to realize your dream will keep you moving forward. True burning desires are simply the unexpressed possibilities within you, as they endeavor to express themselves through your efforts in physical form.

Years ago, a young man asked a wise old man how he could make his dreams come true. The old man said, "Follow me." He led the young man to a river, where he pushed the boy's head under the water, held it there until the lad was flailing about for air, then released him and looked into his eyes. When the young man caught his breath, the old man asked him, "What did you desire most when you were underwater?"

"I wanted air," the young man said.

The old man told him, "When you want your dream as much as you wanted air, you will be on your way to living it."

Now, that is a true burning desire. How much do you want what you say you want? Do you want it badly enough to do whatever it takes to get it? Are you willing to give up whatever's necessary to get it, as the boy would have gladly done to get air when his head was held under the water?

The stronger your desire, the easier it will be to achieve your goal. As your desire increases, more events will move in support of it. And, as you do whatever it takes, your goal will turn into physical reality.

You can build your desire through a program of regular dreambuilding. Dreambuilding puts the images of you successfully achieving your goal into your subconscious mind. It then goes to work to help you achieve that goal.

Psychologists tell us that your mind cannot distinguish between a vividly imagined experience and a real one. It reacts to both in the same way. This is a key point in building your desire. By picturing yourself having achieved your goal, you are focusing on it by creating "memories" of having achieved it.

Since your mind will envision you having lived your dream, it will naturally cause you to act "as if" you've achieved it. When you think, talk and do like a goal-achiever, you'll eventually become one.

Track Your Results

You now have a concise, powerful game plan. You've mastered the basics: You've recruited the power of your subconscious mind, and you're executing your Goal-Achievement Daily Action Plan. Now you need to check the scorecard and see just how well you're doing!

That's where your Dream Goal Tracking System comes in. Without a scorecard, you won't know whether you're winning or losing. You could think you're winning when you're not. The scorecard allows you to measure your progress and determine where you are in the process. It also serves as a guidepost for refining your behaviors so you can achieve your goal more quickly and more easily. Follow these principles when designing your Dream Goal Tracking System:

♦ **Compare your goals and your progress to your own benchmarks.** What others can do or have done isn't important here. You're uniquely different from every other person who has ever lived.

No one else has exactly the same set of abilities, values, and beliefs as you do. Therefore, you can't accurately compare yourself against anyone else. Besides, comparison hurts your self-esteem. It's not fair to yourself to do it. To do so would be to fall into the classic "comparing apples to oranges" trap. Remember, compare yourself, as you were or are, only with yourself as you want to be.

♦ **Invest your time wisely.** This is the most valuable thing you can *invest.*" Two of the best daily time investments you can make are a few minutes given to planning quiet contemplation of your goals. Make this a regular part of your day. *Time given to focused thought about what you need to do next to achieve your goals is perhaps the key to your success.* It helps you use your precious moments to focus on your Dream Goal. If you don't focus on your dream, you just might find yourself frantically climbing the "ladder of success" only to find it's leaning against the wrong wall!

♦ **Reward results, not activity.** You learned earlier that you need to set up a series of milestones on the way to your Dream Goal and then reward yourself for achieving them. You may congratulate yourself each day for completing your Goal-Achievement Daily Activities, but only reward results, not activity.

Spending several hours one day on your Dream Goal is worthless unless they were spent on goal-achieving activities that gave you results. You could spend many hours being busy every day, for the next 10 years, and never make any progress. If you are shuffling papers, "getting ready" to do something, making trivial phone calls, and other "non-goal-achieving/purely maintenance" activities you won't get anywhere. You'll achieve your goal quicker when you work only on goal-achieving activities that produce results.

These three principles—1) compare yourself only to your own benchmarks; 2) use your time wisely; and 3) reward results, not activity—will give you the basis for a sound goal-achievement scorecard. Here's how to put them together to create your ideal tracking system:

Use a Time Log to Keep You on Track to Your Dream Goal

How many hours a week, on average, do you invest doing high-level activities that contribute directly to achieving your Dream Goal? Do you have a pretty good idea? Maybe not.

And if you guess, I would almost guarantee that your guess is much higher than the actual number. Why?

You might not realize how much time you spend needlessly on trivial activities. Things like getting ready in the morning, taking coffee breaks, calling friends, reading the paper, sorting mail, and other mundane tasks, don't contribute directly to achieving your dreams and goals. To accomplish them, you need to do things that would contribute to their realization. Perhaps the following piece by Berton Bradley will inspire you:

> *"If you want a thing bad enough to go out and fight for it, to work day and night for it, to give up your time, your peace and your sleep for it...if all that you dream and scheme is about it, and life seems useless and worthless without it...if you gladly sweat for it and fret for it and plan for it and lose all your terror of the opposition for it...if you simply go after that thing you want with all of your capacity, strength and sagacity, faith, hope and confidence and stern pertinacity...if neither cold, poverty, famine, nor gout, sickness nor pain, of body and brain, can keep you away from the thing that you want...if dogged and grim you beseech and beset it, with the help of God, you WILL get it!"*

Do you want to maximize the speed of your journey toward your dream? Then you *must* know exactly how you're using your time now and where you need to be investing your time from now on.

Keeping a daily time log will make this easy. Here's how to do it:

♦ Get a sheet of blank paper, preferably graph paper. Across one side of the sheet, list the top-priority activities in your life. For example, being with the family, meeting new people, attending seminars, reading a positive book, listening to positive tapes, exercising, and reviewing and visualizing your goals.

♦ Down the other side of the paper, write the dates of the next 21 days. Carry this sheet with you wherever you go and, during the next 21 days, record the productive time you actually had each day. For example, when you invest 20 minutes reading from a positive book, enter 20 minutes in your log. Record only the time you actually read.

♦ Follow this same procedure for all your activities during the next 21 days. Be serious about it and honest with yourself. Time spent on maintenance activities, like organizing your work area, *doesn't* count as productive work time. Time spent drinking coffee and casually daydreaming doesn't count as productive, either. Also, time spent watching TV doesn't count as productive, whether you're with your family or alone.

The average American actually spends only 30 hours a week working on the job, 10 hours at work doing non-work activities (like coffee breaks), 37 hours watching TV, 13 hours in social activities, 42 hours sleeping, and 36 hours in unstructured time and maintenance activities such as eating, showering, and doing errands. Of the 30 hours spent working, only about 8-10 are actually good, solid uninterrupted highly creative hours used for completing goal-achieving activities. If you don't live in the U.S., you may have similar statistics in your country.

What you want to do is get an idea of how many hours in a week you are actually doing productive, goal-achieving activities. You'll also learn how many hours you're spending in routine, non-goal-achieving activities such as getting ready for work, commuting, chatting with friends, piddling around the house, or running errands. These everyday activities are obviously not the best use of your time. Therefore, they need to be your first targets for streamlining, elimination, or delegation, whenever possible.

If you're like most people who do this exercise, you'll probably be shocked at how few productive hours you actually have in a given week. You'll be amazed at how those non-productive hours add up over the course of the year—hours that could have been invested to secure your future.

If you spend one hour each day getting ready for work and another hour commuting (½-hour each way), that's 20 hours a week. That adds up to 1,000 hours a year, or the equivalent of about 24 full work weeks. People always ask me how I get so much done when it seems like I never work. Well, just by working out of my home office, which you may be able to do too, I've gained 1,000 hours per year in otherwise unproductive time.

Your goal with any nonproductive activity that can't be eliminated, at least not right now, is to transform it into productive time that'll help you reach your Dream Goal. For example, you could put a cassette player in your bathroom and listen to positive tapes while you're getting ready for work. You could also turn your car into a "university on wheels" and listen to these tapes on your commute to and from work.

By investing those 1,000+ hours listening to tapes, you'll have the equivalent of two full years of college education in your business or profession! You'll be surprised at how much quicker you can move toward your goals when you listen to one or more of these tapes every day. Listening to the same tape over and over helps you considerably to increase your retention of the information. It'll help you to stay fired up and on track. You can be sure that leaders in your field have listened to a lot of these tapes over the years to help them get to where they are!

Remember take stock of how you're spending your time. Until you know how you're using your time now, you won't know what areas you need to fine-tune so you can achieve your goals in a quicker and easier manner. For example, notice what you're now doing with "waiting" time. Say you're waiting to see your doctor, waiting for the mechanic to finish fixing your car, or waiting for a meeting to start. How are you using that time? Do you pick up whatever's available in the area you're waiting in, like a newspaper or magazine, or do you have a positive book with you to read? Or are you becoming acquainted with the person who's sitting next to you? Are you investing your time wisely? *Always keep a positive book with you to read for those times when you have to wait. Or use the time to make a new acquaintance.*

♦ **Always be as efficient and effective as possible.** Always have a prospect list with you and make good use of the convenience of the phone. Get yourself a day planner and use it every day. Be aware of community activities so you can consistently meet new people. And be sure to counsel with your leader or mentor to help you stay on track.

Be serious about your dream. And, treat your goal-achievement process as if you were the CEO (Chief Executive Officer) of your own multi-million dollar corporation. Think strategically, just as if you're in charge of setting things up to make sure you reach your goals in the speediest, easiest, and best possible manner.

Track Your Progress

One of the most important systems you can set up is a tracking system to measure your progress toward your goal. You've already created a daily time log, so you now know how you're investing your time in moving closer to your goal. The next step is to create a system to track the results your investment of time is giving you. Here is how to do that:

♦ Once again, get a clean sheet of paper, preferably graph paper. Write your Dream Goal in bold letters across the top. Then place the date when you'd like to achieve it, in bold letters in the upper right hand corner. Under your

Dream Goal, write, "Reasons Why" and then describe, in detail, all the benefits you'll receive from achieving it. Then make a box and title it, "Reward," and describe in detail the reward you will give yourself for achieving your Dream Goal. For example, if your goal is to earn $1,000,000 or more, your reward might be a trip around the world or a beautiful new home.

♦ Next, create a section titled, "Steps to Complete." Fill in the first step you need to take to get you closer to your Dream Goal and the date you'll take it. If you've already completed some of the steps, fill them in and then place check marks next to them to indicate they're finished. Next to the date column, add a column titled "Reward" and, fill in the smaller rewards that you will give yourself when you complete that step.

If you don't know all the steps you will need to take to achieve your Dream Goal, great. That means it's a lofty goal and well worthy of stretching to achieve. Just fill in whatever steps you do know. Your increased level of awareness will allow you to know what the next step needs to be and you can fill that in when you know it.

Now, you have a simple goal-achievement tracking form that'll keep you on track to achieving your Dream Goals. Review it at least once a day. Concentrate on feeling the emotions associated with achieving your Dream Goal and all the benefits and rewards you'll receive. Such dreambuilding is key to your success.

The second tracking form that'll be helpful is one to chart the completion of your Main Goal-Achievement Activities. The simplest way to do this is to get a sheet of graph paper and, down one side, list your Main Goal-Achievement Activities— say, there are six activities. Then put the next 30 days' dates across the top. You can then track your progress as follows:

Just check off the activities that you complete each day. For example, if you completed all six activities on March 10, put check marks by each activity under the March 10 column on your sheet. At the end of 30 days, total up your check marks for each of your six activities.

You may have 24 check marks "Building your career or business," and 27 check marks for "Investing one hour of quality time with my family." Divide the number of check marks you have into the number of days to get a percentage of the total days that you actually did what you said you'd do. You built your business or career 80 percent (24/30) of the days and spent time with your family 90 percent (27/30) of the days.

This is an easy way to track how you're doing and what areas you need to focus on. If you noticed, for example, that your sponsoring or registration rate wasn't as high as you'd like it to be, you could look at your chart and see that you skipped six days of contacting. This easily explains why you aren't achieving your goal as quickly as you'd like and gives you an easy way to re-focus your time and energy.

In the beginning, you may find that a couple of your key areas don't get finished every day. It sometimes takes a while to form the habit of living at 100 percent every single day. Be confident. You're competing only against yourself, not anyone else. Keeping a chart like this gives you a benchmark so that you can improve. If you only completed one of your "daily half-dozen" 10 times in 30 days, don't get discouraged with yourself for not using the other 20 days as well as you could have. Just focus on your goal-achievement activities and improve your total in the next 30 days.

The key is continuous improvement. If you accomplished one of your key tasks 15 times last month, go for 25 times this month, and then 30 times next month. As long as you're continually improving, you will be consistently moving toward your goal as quickly as you can.

You can live your life joyously, enjoying the process, because you'll know that you're doing the right things at the right time to achieve your goal. You also know that it's only a matter of time until you reach that Dream Goal.

Using a daily activity log, a goal-achievement steps chart, and a Dream Goal-Achievement Activity Tracking Chart makes it easier for you to stay focused on high-level, goal-achieving activities.

Invest in Your Future and Yourself

Champions at every level are aware of *the razor's edge* between winning and losing. They continually invest their time, energy, and money to acquire the experience and education they need to continuously improve their skills. You need to do the same.

One of the most important, and most often overlooked aspects of living your dream is developing a sound personal development program. By reading this book *and* completing the exercises that it suggests, and taking action, you've made a major stride in the right direction. Keep these points in mind when you're putting your program together:

♦ **Personal development precedes personal fulfillment.** This is another area where people confuse the law of cause and effect. Personal development is the cause; personal fulfillment is the effect. You need to first work on the cause before you can expect the effect to happen.

♦ **Balance your production with improving your ability to produce.** Time is the one constant in your life. We all have 24 hours each day—no more, no less. And no one has any spare time! You need to *invest* a portion of this time in developing yourself so that you can learn how to do more in less time. Say you don't make this investment in personal development and instead spend all your time in production (work). You'd then be locking yourself in to the same level of production for the rest of your life because you wouldn't be learning to grow and improve. You'd also be missing out on much of the joy in life that comes from learning new skills and developing higher levels of understanding.

♦ **Work as hard and smart on yourself as you do on your goal-achieving task at hand.** Which one is more important—becoming a more highly developed person or becoming a better producer? The truth is, becoming a more developed person automatically makes you better at achieving your goals. You'll find yourself able to do more with less effort and earn more money in less time. Growing yourself is the most profitable thing you can do!

Your Very Own Gold Mine

Create your own intellectual, financial, and spiritual feast by setting up a regular program of personal development. The average person in the U.S. spends about 6 percent of their income on food and 12 percent on automobile expenses, but almost nothing on personal development! If you live in another country, depending on the culture, environment, and economy, you may have similar statistics. Some people say they can't afford to buy books or tapes or attend seminars. The truth is they can't afford not to! Think of it this way:

If I came to you and told you that you had an incredible gold mine in your backyard, but it would cost $1,000 for special tools to mine the gold, would you go out and find a way to come up with the $1,000? Of course you would.

That's the same way the "gold mine" in your head works. It's not limited to helping you create just a few golden nuggets, though. Instead it can create immense boulders of wealth—*after* you invest in the special "tools" that you need to develop your mind-mine! *Set aside some funds every month to use for developing yourself. It's key to success!*

♦ *Emphasize BE over BUY.* Invest your money in things that will help you become a more developed person. Buying things that only serve to give the appearance of having become such a person is like living a lie. You may fool some people, but you can't fool yourself. Invest your money wisely and you'll eventually be able to buy whatever you want.

♦ Your own personal development is *the best* long-term investment you'll ever make. Investing in yourself will give you tremendous dividends for the rest of your life— not only financially, but mentally and spiritually as well. You'll also gain a better understanding of yourself and the world around you, leading to healthier relationships. Most importantly, regular personal development assures you are continually growing and moving in the direction of your dream. And remember, you're either growing or rotting. There's no such thing as status quo. If you're not moving on, you're going backward, sabotaging your own success.

Here are some key areas to include in your personal development program:

♦ **Invest in positive books and tapes on a regular basis.** For a minimal cost, a book or tape can give you the chance to enter the minds of some of the world's greatest thinkers and leaders. You'll get to read about and listen to people who are where you want to be. Successful people, who once were at "the bottom" tell their stories and what they learned about success, on tapes you can play over and over. Be sure to listen to at least one such tape a day.

Read books *actively*, highlighting key points you want to remember. And when you've finished reading a book, go back and reread your highlighted portions. This will reinforce the ideas that impacted you most. You may want to write them in your planner or a notebook for even more impact.

The average person in the U.S. reads less than one book a year and 58 percent of Americans never finish a book after high school. If you live elsewhere, do you know the statistics for your country? Will you beat them?

Reading 15-20 minutes a day will give you an incredible edge over almost everyone else. If you read one book a month for five years, you will have digested the wisdom of 60 books. What a difference this can make in your life!

Who has the advantage—you, the reader—or most people, the nonreaders? As the saying goes, *leaders are readers. Read today, lead tomorrow.*

♦ **Attend seminars regularly.** They give you the chance to learn from the most successful people in your field—live. They can give you hope and maybe even the key that opens the door to achieving your Dream Goal more quickly and easily than you ever thought possible. Another benefit of attending seminars is associating with other positive thinking people who are also moving on. They'll help you to stay motivated.

Enjoy the Process—*The Journey IS the Success!*

Remember, enjoy your life to the absolute maximum. Be happy now because now is all you have. Yesterday is history and tomorrow is promised to no one! Have fun with the journey of success and confidently move forward every day to achieve your Dream Goal. As William Shakespeare once said, *"No profit grows where there is no pleasure taken."* Take pleasure in all you've accomplished so far and all you'll accomplish in the future. Stop for a minute and reflect on how far you've come to date. Enjoy the process as you move on to *"The Final Frontier."*

Chapter 14

Work With A Leadership "Success Coach" To Help Keep You Focused On Achieving Your Dream Goal

> *"Lives of great men [and women] all remind us we can make our lives sublime [noble]; and departing, leave behind us, footprints on the sands of time."*
> Henry Wadsworth Longfellow

Success—*The Final Frontier*

Congratulations! You're right on track to be one of the few people in the world who can truly say they're living their goals and living their dreams. That's exciting, isn't it? You have only two more steps to go—

1. Duplicate other winners.
2. Work with a leadership "Success Coach" to keep you focused and on track toward achieving your Dream Goal.

Duplicate Other Winners

One of the most powerful ways to stay focused on achieving your Dream Goal is to model other champions who have already achieved what you're aiming for. You may or may not know these people personally. You may have seen them briefly at a seminar or read about them a magazine. Maybe you have a tape of them speaking and sharing how they succeeded.. You can still learn from them through reading about or listening to them. You can learn where they started and how far they've come on their journey by checking out their biographies. Talk to other people who know them and, if possible, observe how they respond to different situations. Duplicate what other winners do and you can also achieve the level of success they've achieved.

Find people who have overcome their fears and learn from them. Find people who have done what you want to do and model them. Find people who have the qualities you want to develop and who are like the kind of person you want to become. Associate with people who have goals and dreams and spend time with them. Learn about them and from them as much as you can. The company you keep plays a major role in determining the way you look at the world and the actions you take. So, associate with winners.

Who do you spend time with now? How are these people affecting you? Is your association with these people supporting you in moving you closer to your Dream Goal, or is it keeping you from achieving your goal? Do these people support and encourage you or tear you down? Do they want you to succeed or do they want you to follow the crowd that's going nowhere fast, perhaps, like them? Do they invest their time wisely growing and building for the future or re-living the past? Are they basically in a survival mode—just "getting by"—rather than getting a new life?

Associate with People Who Focus on Goals and Dreams, Not Problems.

If you hang around with people who aren't growing and becoming, it's not likely you'll ever grow and become either.

Your role models will be people with negative thinking. You'll find yourself complaining about everything and anything with a "victim" mentality. Your thoughts will dwell on negativity. You will look in the mirror and see an unhappy person. You will get put down every time you do something that threatens the identity of the miserable group you're hanging out with. You will be like most people—like a hamster running in a circular cage—going nowhere fast.

If you hang around with a bunch of people who, for instance, refuse to move on with their lives, your role models will be these uninspiring people. You'll think about the same old stuff. You'll look in the mirror and see yourself as just growing older—not better. You'll remain stuck. As difficult as it may be, you need to quit spending time with people who have the same problems as you do and who aren't doing anything about them.

You also need to—*quit spending time with people who don't support you in achieving your goals and dreams.* The balance between mental thoughts and physical reality is incredibly close. Don't take a chance that the naysayers you know will attempt to steal your precious dreams. But don't make a big deal out of it. Just begin replacing your old negative acquaintances with new positive ones who encourage and uplift you. Soon you will be surrounded by a group of champions, just like yourself. And when a pack of champions bursts out of the gate, there's no stopping them on the way to victory!

Everyone Needs a Mentor and a Success Partner

Another extremely effective way to stay on track to your Dream Goal is to find a mentor and a success partner.

A mentor is someone who's done what you'd like to do. They can counsel you to help you avoid the pitfalls along the way, and help keep you on track. They can also introduce you to other successful people as well. When you find someone who you'd like to have as your mentor, don't be afraid to ask them. Most successful people are complimented that you value their opinion and would probably be happy to share their ideas with you. If they can't help you, ask if they know someone you could approach.

Don't expect your mentor to be a perfect role model in every area. We all have our strengths and weaknesses. It's perfectly acceptable, and in fact I would strongly recommend, that you have different mentors for different areas of your life. Pick the best person in each area and then learn from them. That way you're getting the best of the best at all times.

One mentor could be a priest, pastor or rabbi. This person, who could help you develop spiritually, is unlikely to be able to help you achieve your Dream Goal. You'll need to look to someone who is successful in your field for that kind of counseling. That's perfectly fine. Just realize one person is unlikely to be your mentor for everything. Everyone has different experience and expertise.

A success partner is another key person to build a solid relationship with. This could be your spouse or maybe more successful business associate. A success partner is someone who shares your love of learning and growing. If this person is your spouse, the two of you will share your goals and commit to helping each other achieve them.

Success partners are accountable to each other for taking goal-achieving action daily. They need to give you key support in keeping your dreams alive and encouraging you.

Mike Fry, president of Total Sports Photography and Fancy Fortune Cookies, is my own success partner. While I was writing this book, we called each other every morning and went over our goals for the day. We kept each other accountable for actually doing every day what we said we were going to do.

If one of us wasn't doing what we needed to, we got on each other's "case" a bit. Strongly, yet in a positive way, we'd help the other one get back on track. We reminded each other of all the great things and people that we were attracting to us as we achieved our goals. And, when something good happened, we were on the phone to share it with each other immediately. This kind of partnership made a huge difference in our success. I strongly recommend you find a success partner to help you turn your dreams into reality.

All Champions Have Coaches

Think for a minute about top athletes like Michael Jordan, Tiger Woods, Cal Ripken, Mark McGwire, and others. What comes to your mind? World-class performance, right? Now, think for another minute about how they got that way. The answer is simple: they all have coaches who helped them stay focused and on track. These coaches also provided, with the increasingly fine distinctions, like assistance with skills and attitude development, that separate the champions from the rest of the world.

Why should you be any different? There's absolutely no reason you shouldn't have a Success Coach. We all need someone who'll help you stay on track and provide us with the fine-tunings that will help us realize our Dream Goal. We all need someone who can get us to do what we otherwise wouldn't.

American writer and humorist, Mark Twain, said it best— *"Keep away from people who try to belittle your ambitions. Small people always do that, but the really great make you feel that you, too, can become great."*

Is This the End? No! It's Only the Beginning...

Congratulations! You've really come a long way since the start of this book. You're now at a crossroads—the end of your old life—the beginning of a new life full of happiness, wealth, and success.

You need to continue doing whatever it takes as you execute your Dream Goal-Achievement Daily Action Plan. Keep fine-tuning your skills, focusing on distinctions that give you *the razor's edge.* You need to combine those things with a positive mental attitude. You need to continue developing by feeding your mind with the right "food"— books, tapes, seminars, and other success-developing activities. As you persist toward your Dream Goal, you'll soon be joining the ranks of the champions.

Now, before I go, I want to leave you with one thought that sums up what the entire goal-achievement process is all about: *"The highest reward for a person's toil is not what they get for it, but what they become by it."* Keep growing and becoming more of the person you want to be each day!

Best wishes for a richly rewarding, thoroughly enjoyable, marvelously successful journey. Remember, focus on your dream and make it yours! As Lee Iacocca, former CEO of Chrysler Corporation, once said...

*"The ability
to
concentrate
—focus—
and use
your time well
is
everything."*

ABOUT THE AUTHOR

Jeff Smith is the executive director of The Center for Personal Excellence. He coaches top entrepreneurs in many fields to grow their businesses and achieve their personal and professional goals while leading healthy, balanced, low-stress lives. He lives in New Mexico. He's been a frequent guest on radio and TV programs nationwide in the U.S. He also speaks at seminars and conducts live training sessions based on the principles in this book.